Light & Shade

Light & Shade

NEW AND SELECTED POEMS

Tom Clark

Introduction by Amy Gerstler

Coffee House Press
Minneapolis
2006

COPYRIGHT © 2006 Tom Clark
COVER & BOOK DESIGN Linda S. Koutsky
COVER PAINTING *Retirement*, 1981 © Tom Clark
AUTHOR PHOTOGRAPH © Mark Gould

Coffee House Press books are available to the trade through our primary distributor, Consortium Book Sales & Distribution, 1045 Westgate Drive, Saint Paul, MN 55114. For personal orders, catalogs, or other information, write to: Coffee House Press, 27 North Fourth Street, Suite 400, Minneapolis, MN 55401.

Coffee House Press is a nonprofit literary publishing house. Support from private foundations, corporate giving programs, government programs, and generous individuals help make the publication of our books possible. We gratefully acknowledge their support in detail in the back of this book.

Good books are brewing at coffeehousepress.org

LIBRARY OF CONGRESS CATALOGING-IN-PUBLICATION DATA

Clark, Tom, 1941–
Light and shade : new and selected poems / Tom Clark ;
introduction by Amy
Gerstler.
p. cm.
ISBN-13: 978-1-56689-183-7 (alk. paper)
ISBN-10: 1-56689-183-3 (alk. paper)
I. Title.
PS3553.L29L54 2006
811'.54—DC22
2005035810

FIRST EDITION | FIRST PRINTING
1 3 5 7 9 8 6 4 2
Printed in Canada

To Angelica, always

Contents

I   Author's Note
III   Introduction:
    "Tom Clark's Heart," by Amy Gerstler

1963–1968

1   "Like musical instruments . . ."
2   A Difference
3   Eyeglasses
4   A Winter Day
6   The Knot
8   Doors
11   You (I)
12   You (II)
14   You (III)
15   You (IV)
16   You (V) (after Hölderlin)
18   Easter Sunday
19   "Als Kind verliert sich eins im stilln . . ."
20   Dark Continent
21   A Lamp
22   A Red Wild Flower in North Africa
23   Hitching
24   The Yearbook
25   Change
26   Afternoons
27   And Now to the Stars
28   Momentum
29   Explanatory Ways
30   Sunglasses
31   Going to School in France or America

32 A Crazy American Girl

33 Penmanship

35 Superballs

36 I'm on an Island

37 Daily News

38 Sonnet

39 The Lake

43 Where I Live

44 "My heart in pieces . . ."

1968–1978

47 Now She Dwells Here

48 Pillow

49 One

50 Nimble Rays of Day Bring Oxygen to Her
Blood

51 Up in Here

52 Short Order

53 Air

54 Things About You

56 80°

57 A Perfect Stranger

58 Locations

60 Hush, Hush

61 Slow Life

62 August 6, 1969

63 Magic Arrival No. 7

64 Crows

65 Back to the Front

66 The Tire

67 Eos

68 Sky

69 The Greeks

70 The Byrds

71 Bugs Ate This Lake Clean

78 Paper People

79 Nouns

80 Nothing Inside

81 Things to Watch Out For in California

82 Brainards

83 Novel

84 Heavy

85 from SMACK

93 33 Statements

95 Safari

96 Imagine

97 Whistle Buoy

98 Life Notes

99 Ah—There

100 The Door to the Forest

101 Hot Dog

102 Poetry Street

103 Campaign

104 Evolution

105 On Venus

106 Water

107 One More Saturday Night

108 The Stars

109 Breadwinning

112 Baseball & Classicism

113 Radio

117 Nine Songs

119 from SUITE

122 And Don't Ever Forget It

123 I Was Born to Speak Your Name

125 Every Day

126 Gift of Tongue

127 Jan. 8

128   Birds

129   Euphrates River

130   A New Light

131   Gale

132   Winter Storm on Alder Road

134   Realism

135   October

136   The Big Cigars

137   So Long

138   35

139   Hot Agate

140   Life Flowed Between Us

141   The Great One

142   Clemente (1934-1972)

143   To Ungaretti

145   The Last Poem (after Robert Desnos)

146   Love (after La Rochefoucauld)

147   The Color of Stepped On Gum

148   Crisis on the Savannah

149   Moving Out

1978–1987

153   Mountain Men

154   Boulder

155   The Light of the World at 9000 Feet

156   War

157   A Trip to Erie and Hygiene

158   No Tears for Buccaneers

159   A Missing Child

160   Secrets of the Estate

161   After the Slide

162   Following Rivers into the Night

163   Population Control in Gillette

164 Wyoming

165 "All I want to do . . ."

166 The Nike of Boone

168 What the Pioneers Always Wanted to Do Was
     Arrive

169 Heartbreak Hotel

171 The Nelsons in San Roque

172 Things to Do in California (1980)

173 The Class Doesn't Struggle Anymore

174 Another Exotic Introduction

175 The Pack Approaches the Mission

177 Under the Fortune Palms

178 Off Goleta

179 Dear Customer

180 More Crooked Lines from Paradise

181 A Polyester Notion

182 Lines Composed at Hope Ranch

183 The Muses' Exodus

184 "Those men whom the gods wish . . ."

185 Sadly Céline

186 Wrong from the Start

187 Identification Tags

188 Teflon and Velcro

189 Say What?

190 Democracy

191 January 25

192 The Blue Dress

1987–1995

195 Arctic Cold Snap

196 The Possessed Winter Dusk

197 Solstice

198 Fractured Karma

199 Eternity Time Share Rebus

200 Seduction in the Wider Fields of Eternity
201 Perishable Memo
202 Aqualung
203 Subject
204 Tree Talk
205 Inside the Redwood
206 Linnaeus' Flower Clock
207 For Robert Duncan
208 As the Human Village Prepares for Its Fate
209 The Lyric
210 Statue
211 Nodding
212 Energy of the Pre-World as a Bungee Cable Jumper
213 Antiquarian
214 Moira
215 Day Detail—Low Light of Afternoon
216 "First cold winter twilights . . ."
217 Final Farewell
218 Possession
219 Premonitory (Keats, Teignmouth, Spring 1818)
221 Phosphorescence (Keats, Hampstead, May 1819)
222 Weight (Keats, Winchester, September 1819)
223 Melancholy Watch, the Downs (Keats, September 1820)
224 Keats: Coda: Echo and Variation
231 Like Real People
232 Getaway Package
233 Happy Talk
234 Christmas on Telegraph
235 Through This Long Winter of Freakshows and Floods
236 To the Mistress of the Sailor's Rest

237 Old Album

238 On the Beach

239 Torn from an Old Album

1995–2005

243 from EMPIRE OF SKIN

252 Earthshine

253 On the Playing Fields

254 Prolepsis

255 Elegy

256 Surrender

259 Trinity

260 Childhood

261 Little Bang

262 Light Sleeper

263 Out of the Fog

264 Children of the Future

265 Footsteps

266 Bach's Booty

267 To the Muses of a Certain Age

268 Night Sky (March 23, 1997)

270 from COLD SPRING: A DIARY

275 For Ed Dorn

276 Farewell Sweet Prince

277 The Spell

278 Another Obscure Reverie

279 Little Hymn to Athene

280 All Thought

281 Drifting

282 Hope

283 Vagabondage

284 Message in the Fog

285 Vow

286 In Water World

287 Intermittent Tempest

288 The Day Goes on Forever

289 All Souls

290 Another Sleepless Night

292 Why Hillary Became a Goddess on the Night of Her Acceptance Speech

294 Venerable Imp Rebus

295 Bookmark

296 Phil

297 All

299 Memories at Dawn

302 Ann Arbor 1960

303 At Life

304 The Key

305 Lullaby for Cuckoo

306 A Fairy Tale

307 Les Etoiles

308 Night Sky

309 Hazard Response

310 The Pilots

311 November of the Plague Year

312 Everything Makes Sense If You Close Your Eyes and Let It

313 Halloween of Double Happiness

314 Lustration Rite

315 Nux

316 The Great Sphinx Who Rests With Paws

317 Empty Message File

318 Species

319 All Souls Night

320 The Vacant Estate

321 Chiasmus

322 White Dove

323 The Maid

324 Beauty

325 Prophet

326 Adversary

327 The Two Lords

328 As If Anything Could Happen

329 In the Time of the Smoking Mirror

330 Post-Election

331 The Course of Empire Unwinds

332 Sunflowers

335 Selected Bibliography

338 Acknowledgments

Light and Shade: Author's Note

This collection of poems written over five decades originally bore the title *Night Sky*. Two of the individual pieces here retain that as their title; the latter parts of the book indeed contain many night pieces, perhaps naturally so, as these parts arise from a largely nocturnal life—just as earlier parts of the book can be seen to contain many pieces that reflect the plainer yet more variegated lights of day, as naturally prevailing in the less somber morning and afternoon of a life.

As to the phrase "light and shade," no one who has attended even a little while to the craft aspect of poetry is likely to forget the quiet but firm response of a dying John Keats to a friend's entreaty that he write more poetry: without one's physical health, the doomed young man politely answered, one lacked the necessary wherewithal for poetry—that "primitive information, light and shade," which, Keats succinctly explained, comprised for him the essential source of lyric composition.

Also hovering around the background of not only the present work's title but much of its contents is an idea of lyric poetry as a play of light that is not general and ambient but partial, selective and emanating from a single rather fragile source, like a solitary candle flame in the paintings of the seventeenth-century shadowmaster Georges de la Tour, which illuminates some of the common objects and scenes around it while leaving others—often at least equally significant—clothed in darkness and invisibility. The solitude of a consciousness at the center of a meditative space in that moment in which a single fragment of time is bathed: the poem's flickering spark lights up what is admittedly a small world of subjective revelation, beyond which lies a larger obscurity, the shadow-play of death's immanence in life.

Tom Clark's Heart

Tom Clark is a great American lyric poet. To those of us who care about such things, that makes him something of a national treasure. Readers fond of literary labels and jargon might peg him as a latter-day practitioner of *lyrisme romantique,* the definition of which seems to (almost) perfectly characterize his poems:

> A term used to describe those qualities of French lyrical poetry which appeared to depend greatly upon the individual poet's personal experiences and feelings. . . . The four major poets of the French Romantic movement . . . 'wrote from the heart.'[i]

Though Clark was born in 1941 (not 1802 like Victor Hugo) and in Chicago (not France, though his watershed stint as editor of *The Paris Review* might qualify him as an honorary Frenchman) it is the word "heart" and the concept of *heart* in poetry I want to emphasize here. That word and idea appear in so many panged and brooding, giddy and melancholy, ardent and wracked conjugations in the pages you are about to read. Since *Light and Shade* takes its title from Keats, as Clark tells us in his author's note, I will add another Keats quote, very closely descriptive of the sensibility in these poems: "I am certain of nothing but the holiness of the Heart's affections and the truth of Imagination."[ii]

Clark's humane, visionary lyrics convey both bounce and gravity. *The heart as a rubber ball.* His is an idealistic, sad, gorgeous, intelligent voice, funny, and at times gymnastic. He's a wit, a romantic, and a compassionate thinker. His poems make the reader feel "spiritual and alert." They are as graceful as Fred Astaire, and can be goofy within the same moves, just as Astaire could be. Clark understands what Astaire knew in his muscles and bones, that real grace fuses elements of rigor and play.

Because these poems span forty some years, there is great delight to be had in tracing an intensely talented poet's trajectory from early boyish verve, and drunkenness on both the classical and the vernacular, through the ups and downs of husbandhood, fatherhood, locations and relocations, the loss of parents and friends, and on into the bumpy surprises and vagaries of middle age. Additionally, since he began writing, Clark has now and then taken on the laudable but unenviable job (remember Cassandra?) of being a conscience of his times. I don't think he embraced this role voluntarily. It is simply his lot and his fate and we are the better for it. He takes the predicament of America in this millennium as personally as he has always taken other pressing quandaries of being human. He takes our crazy, untenable situation *to heart.*

Clark's abiding interests are well represented here. Like Marianne Moore, he's a keen appreciator of that most lyrical of sports: baseball (see his two beautiful elegies for Roberto Clemente). His taste in music is eclectic. John Lennon, Miles Davis, Neil Young, The Byrds, Bach, Jimmy Reed, Ray Charles, Henry Purcell, Leadbelly, and Bob Dylan make cameo appearances. A painter himself, Clark's involvement with visual art can be gleaned from reading "33 Statements": a tart, comic send up of aesthetic criticality. And as was the case with T. S. Eliot, Thomas Gray, and Christopher Smart, cats occasionally play pivotal roles in Clark poems. Though I am mostly a dog person myself, I cannot reread the handful of elegies for felines in this book without weeping. *Light and Shade* also contains some of the most real and moving poems I've seen about love over the long haul—tender and sharp meditations on that rare, undersung terra incognita of growing old together.

Clark's poems constitute a happy marriage (though they are not always cheerful) between classical poetic sensibility and postmodern ache. Back in my youth, he single-handedly convinced me (and continues to do so now) that it was possible to produce poems in the immediate moment that draw on the loveliness and depth-of-feeling of English-language poetry past while simultaneously wrestling with the sometimes harrowing and strangely edited present.

As a kid, Clark had a job ushering baseball games at both Wrigley Field and Comiskey Park. I'll let him tell this, because I just received an e-mail from him (in response to a factual inquiry) and I cannot bear to paraphrase his epistolary prose:

Yes indeed, from '56–'58 (high school years) one had a job with an ushering syndicate (keep in mind this is Chicago, where "syndicate" had/has real meaning) which did crowd control at all major public events. I mean all. That is yes, baseball games . . . but also football games (Chicago Bears), race tracks (Arlington Park, Washington Park), professional wrestling (actually a form of theatre, usually at ancient derelict arena next door to vast putrid stockyards), roller derby(!), boxing (Chicago Stadium—e.g. Sugar Ray Robinson vs. Gene Fullmer championship fight), hockey (Blackhawks), trade conventions, political conventions (hello Harry Truman and Madame Chiang Kai-shek), neighborhood dances (brick hits you in the head, all in line of duty), etc. etc. As you can probably imagine all of that work with and for "the public" involved a certain steady and continuous exposure to the basic facts of life, thus was educational in a sense (also no doubt deforming in a sense—but then, what else is any kind of education). What was gained was a huge unsorted store of folkloric and proto-cultural data; also, perhaps, now that I think of it, a certain aversion to crowds. As to later experiences, hmm . . . probably fewer "literary scenes" than survival scenes, learning scenes and scenes of wandering and wondering. Five universities. Various exhausting travels on three continents back when it was possible to be a world citizen even if you were an American and had no money. Then a hundred years go by and here we are. Angelica warns me not to go on about this, as you're (luckily) not writing my life story.

Clark attended the University of Michigan and then Cambridge University on a Fulbright. At the tender age of twenty-two he became poetry editor of *The Paris Review,* on the recommendation of his former teacher Donald Hall, and held that post from 1963 to 1973. With Clark at the helm, the magazine published Allen Ginsberg, Barbara Guest, John Ashbery, Lorine Niedecker, Ed Dorn, Amiri Baraka, James Schuyler, Kenward Elmslie, Lou Reed, Robert Creeley, Ted Berrigan, Ron Padgett, Joanne Kyger, Lorenzo Thomas, Ed Sanders, Anne Waldman, Charles Olson, Alice Notley,

Jim Carroll, Edwin Denby, John Wieners, Frank O'Hara (though sadly not during his lifetime) and many more "big cigars" in the poetry world. Despite his slight disclaimer above, by all reports, Clark did make the literary scenes in England, Bolinas, NYC, Naropa, and now lives semi-incognito in Berkeley with his lovely wife Angelica, slaving away while the muse lashes him daily.

I know of no poet more wholly committed to his practice, despite the fact that this has meant that over the decades this book spans, Clark has had to cobble together (in his words) a "living by my wits, with no secure academic position to fall back on."[iii] Thus stubbornly devoted to the cause of poetry (to the detriment of his own comfort in life, as is often the case) Clark is also frighteningly prolific. His complete bibliography must log in currently somewhere around a zillion volumes, or at any rate it's way, way up there, and the meter's still running. Yet unlike many who churn out stacks of books in multiple genres, his entire output is completely worth reading.

If all this sounds less like a scholarly book intro than a blatant rave, an unstopped gush, the soppy droolings of a rabid fan, well, hand me a towel and congratulate yourself, dear reader. You were quick to figure that out. Check out not only his poems conveniently selected and chronologically arrayed for you here, and his lively criticism and fiction but also his biographies of Damon Runyon, Jack Kerouac, Charles Olson, Ted Berrigan, and others; or begin a rereading campaign if you are already among the converted. Alice Notley described Clark's work as, "a pure arena for the imagination to play in . . . Clark is likewise pure, austere, bleak, exalted too." He's a master of the passionate, beautifully agonized utterance. I'm sorry about this gaga rant, but it does come from the heart, and you get the message: Tom Clark is the real thing. Neglect to read him at your own peril.

—*Amy Gerstler*

[i]   J. A. Cuddon ed. *The Penguin Dictionary of Literary Terms and Literary Theory.* Penguin Books, London, 1999.
[ii] Keats's letter of November 22, 1817 quoted from: Walter Jackson Bate. *Criticism: The Major Texts.* Wolf Den Books, Miami, Florida, 2002.
[iii] Interview of Tom Clark by Kevin Ring in *Beat Scene* UK, #42, Autumn 2002. Reprinted in *Jacket* magazine (online) #21. jacketmagazine.com/21/clark-iv1.html.

A shorter version of this piece appeared in *Mississippi Review,* Fall 2003.

Light & Shade

1963–1968

"Like musical instruments . . ."

Like musical instruments
Abandoned in a field
The parts of your feelings

Are starting to know a quiet
The pure conversion of your
Life into art seems destined

Never to occur
You don't mind
You feel spiritual and alert

As the air must feel
Turning into sky aloft and blue
You feel like

You'll never feel like touching anything or anyone
Again
And then you do

A Difference

Something fallen out of the air, some
thing that was breathing there before
stopped: or say it is a difference

felt quickly on turning from one's work
to the window, and seeing there the same
trees the same color, the sky still without clouds,

changed only in reference to the trees
which also seem to have turned away.
The world still external but less distinct

at its center. For a few
seconds. Fall. The centerfielder drifts under
the last fly ball of the summer, and puts it away.

Eyeglasses

Of this house I know the backwindow
lodges six housesparrows in the bricks

Under the sill, and they are the birds
scour these roofs all winter for warmth

Or whatever. Two are arguing now
for a few inches of position on a cornice.

How the mind moves out and lights on things
when the *I* is only a glass for seeing:

I stand at the window

Setting down each bird, roof, chimney
as the boundaries of the neighborhood they make.

I have on an old blue jersey.
Every two hours I wipe off my glasses.

A Winter Day

A winter day, thirty degrees
in the sun, cold

sunset. To say
a flower in a glass

is like the sun, begs
the sufferance of the thing, the

sun. It has been so many times
compared. Instead

to say
today, a winter day

we picked a willow spray,
put it in a glass,

studied the setting out
of its branches.

Thread and fold of the willow,
thin cloth drawing off

your hips and breasts
as you stooped to touch the glass,

and a sufferance
argued, in your eye

suffering my eye to follow.

The Knot

*"L'homme ne'st qu'un noeud de relations,
les relations comptent seules pour l'homme"*
—SAINT-EXUPÉRY

The four of
them together
beneath the roof
of the one
room school—

someone's relative
is in the photograph—

in my hand it breaks, a leaf,
found in a book,

the yellow veins, the brown
split edges. I

imagine them—the four

together—holding
hands; all are

6

dead now. A man
is his relations
with men, he

is strings
coming together

to form a knot,

who has had a hand in it.

Doors

A love that is not pardoned
But burns the hand that touches
The wind
Tears her form out of the corner
Something presses me her voice
Across the sea a light is lifted
A woman walks to the edge
Of the mud in the street clinging to her packages

In the car of the sea these rusted shapes
Take up the night with a music like stone
The door will not close
Smoke   The cotton
Stuffing of the room
Flatness under my feet walking around the room
A weight on my tongue
The stone fenders are close to the water
At any step you might fall
Things are going badly now
Nothing swims up through
The metal that holds the muddy flowers

There is dirt in every space and a cold wind
Comes off the sea
Pleats of the bedclothes make a hole in the light
A dirty shadow on the door above your head

And the wall bends up losing you
We go at different speeds
Side by side while you sleep

It is grey ahead where I am going

It is too hot
All rooms beat constantly
Something is the matter with the doors but no one stops
We rush through the joys that were there
The same weight of confusion leads me
To pick up everything I find
I turn this over in my hand and find you
Your hands are behind your head
Forming a grave on the pillows
Reality only listens when your words are true
How much longer can the door be found
By picking strings
To a chamber where a vestment
Never speaks until the door to the other side
Upward through the mud to the spoons
Has been closed
A chorus of swine lets loose
In a grey corner the rats continue to sing
Most of this is useless
An insane need for genuflecting
The night flaps
I stand at the edge of you
Is there a switch to be turned

To end this bluff against music
Which outshines the diamond in the slush
All of us wanted to have
Are there green parks where bicycles still glide
We sat on the hills quarreling
As you undress the perfection
Of hair marking each part of you
That seeps down through
This maze of pictures
I carry like sections of cloth d'or
In ancient paintings there is a duel in which
There are
Wings beating in something like hay
Beyond which the mystery is encountered again
She replaces the packages under her arms
And walks through the door

You (1)

The door behind me was you
and the radiance, there like
an electric train wreck in your eye
after a horrible evening of waiting outside places in the rain for you to come
only to
find all of them, two I know, the rest scullions, swimming around you
in that smoky crowded room like a fishbowl
I escaped from, running away from you and my André Breton
dream of cutting your breasts off with a trowel
and what does that matter to them or to you now, but just wait it's still early
to the children embroidered in the rug, who seem to be setting up siege
engines under a tree house full of midgets who look like you.
Where are you in this sky of new blue
deltas I see in the drapery, and your new friends wearing bamboo singlets
what are they doing down there in the moat waving tridents like stalks of
    corn?
Me, I'd be happy to see their blood spilled all over the bedspread
pavilions of your hands as an example. If you come home right now I'll
    scrunch your hat
between my thighs like a valentine before you have time to wipe them.

You (II)

You are bright, tremendous, wow.
But it is the hour of one from whom the horrible tremendousness
Of youth is about to depart.
The boats are ready. The air is soft and you perhaps nearby
Do pass, saying "I am for you."
This is as much as "everything is great."
But desperation builds up all the time.
Life is nothing
        more to me
Strapped at the bottom
     of the throat
Than majesty, I think. You are arduous as that
Ashtray. Swallow me! since
Your hands are full of streets
And I walk out upon the streets
And I think the girls are better looking, vicious, cool
And the men are flying kites and newsprint
Gets on my arms. I enter rooms—
Wild my steps like an automaton's—
Where the batons are linked into some residue.
A gull is eating some garbage.
The sky is an old tomato can, I think.
I buy a newspaper and begin to walk back.
Smells torture the kites like gulls. Wild gulls, and
It's the tremendous sky of survival.
Few things are still visible to me. Baseball

Withholds the tremors. They fall, so
I drag you down and
You are akimbo as I stick it in
And everything is thunderous accordion April, great,
Risen from palms and hypnotism. I run home
And dip my coffee in bread, and eat some of it.

You (III)

Today I get this letter from you and the sun
buckles   a mist falls over our villas
with a hideous organic slush like the music of Lawrence Welk
I lay in bed all day, asleep, and like some nocturnal
beast. And get your salutation among the torn green numbers
in the sky over the council houses. And see your eyes when
                                    the retired pensioners pass
me by the abandoned railway station—this is not nothing, it is not
                                    the hymn
of an age of bankrobbers or heraldic days but it is to sing
with complete gaiety until your heart freaks. I love you.
                                    And go down amid the
  sycamores to

summer. Wandering by the lake any way
                                    seems lovely, grand, the moon
is a gland in the thigh. Tumble and twinkle as on the golf course apparel
lifts. And a door is opened to
an owl. It is snowing, and you are here on the bed with me
and it is raining, and I am as full of frets as a guitar or a curtain
and I am singing, as I sponge up the cat place. You
                                    are heaped
the word reminds me of Abydos and spinach. A curtain
of belief keeps me away from the tombs
of imagery. I love you, I'd like to go.

You (IV)

The chords knotted together like insane nouns   Dante
you are in bed   in the dark copula you
of the musical phrase   a few star birds sing in the branches
their voices are tangled not high
now all of them are dark and some move   you
were a word, in the wood of my life
where the leaves are words, some of them fucking
in obscurity their clasping is terrible and brusque
pain birds ache thru them   and some
are lighter and seem to suggest less
of death than of a viola da gamba player these
birds sweep past in the forest
of my hands on your chest,   as we move
out on the glowing sea of the tropics on an ice pack,   you,

You (v)
(after Hölderlin)

O Earth Mother, who consents to everything, who forgives everything
don't hide like this   and tell

Her Power is sweetened in these rays, the Earth before her
      conceals the children
of her breast in her cloak, meanwhile we feel her,

and the days to come announce
that much time has passed and often one has felt
      a heart grow for you inside his chest
They have guessed, the Ancients, the old and pious Patriarchs,
        and in the secret they are, without even knowing it,
        blessed
in the twisted chamber, for you, the silent men
but still more, the hearts, and those you have named Amor,
or have given obscure names, Earth, for one is shamed
to name his inmost heart, and from the start however man
when he finds greatness in himself and if the Most High permits,
He names it, this which belongs to him, and by its proper name
and you are it, and it seems
                to me I hear the father say
to you honor is granted from now on
and you must receive songs in its name,
and you must, while he is distant and Old Eternity
      becomes more and more hidden every day,

take his place in front of mortals, and since
you will bear and raise children for him, his wish
is to send anew and direct toward you men's lives
when you recognize him   but this
directive which he inscribes in me is the rose
Pure sister, where will I get hold, when it is winter, of these
flowers, so as to weave the inhabitants of heaven crowns
                              It will be
as if the spirit of life passed out of me,
because for the heavenly gods these signs
of love are flowers in a desert   I search for them, you are hidden

Easter Sunday

Someone has frozen the many-storeyed houses
Under this planetarium
A brilliant silence like a foghorn

A perfect frieze before the complications
Arrive with dialogue and
The olives of daily life

This brown Barcelona paper
Thrown onto the blue stone of the day
Makes everyone stop leaving

Through the light in a glass of wine you see them
Under the hot sky of the glacier
Placing their bets then boarding the funeral train

"Als Kind verliert sich eins im stilln . . ."

Sometimes children get lost in silence
under the hood of the big bell
we get lost where it is cold and dark
and the escaping bird
breaks its wing against the bell wall
the great rim cracks
a thread of light slips through
we are lost our breath
falters in silence a memorized note and
one day it sings of death
no longer guilty as the rain
we will come back
to the loved earth like flies clothed in snow

Dark Continent

The journey in darkness has a trivial jargon
For the cans of black coffee and ears like sprigs
Of an intelligent listening flower

This agitation is a kind of heavy wood
That you could hold a candle to
And never alter its unendurableness

There is nothing to do about voyaging
Fears except to jerk their brilliance
Out ahead of you like a rushlight like this

But what is illumined in the jungle large
Is a girl in narrow white sashes
Seated in your room at your writing desk

A Lamp

      A lamp too near the floor
in the dim light thought   love   old letters
phone calls

          turn to water
waves of matter like cups and chairs
                            Memories

of places we will never return to and few
of us living in isolated apartments
will speak to each other again in the night

far apart and with our hands over our faces
asleep and looking at the ceiling
under a borrowed blanket

A Red Wild Flower in North Africa

The hand a halo
     does not touch it   it
  wavers

A red wild flower in North Africa
    shimmers

A stone in the wind   the sand
some dust blows in the sun   the wind
stops   we stand by the road
stops blowing   we stand by the road

A leaf blows against the stone

We are standing by the side of a road in the desert
some dust blows against a leaf
we look at it   all day

       the curious
     pelted foldedness
        its livery
      like a candy paper

a poppy?
the wind stops

Hitching

In the photograph in which (just as our drive is starting) we notice that
There were six families in Barking,
Six husbands and six wives (the caption explains that
Now in 1966 they are all alive),
Some children have entered the picture.
One of them may become champion of the world.

The Yearbook

When I began this poem about our directions
Six months ago, there was an ornamental
Fountain six inches from my face

In the book I was reading then, in the room
Where the six of us had been,
Robert, Larry, Anita, Eve and me,

And the other, whose role never
Came clear to me till tonight; even
Now I do not know his name

So let's forget about him!

Change

Stepping down was like being born
out of the flank
of a bus, like Dionysus from
Zeus. The guts of the pavement
lay open under flags and gazers.

As we passed the bank and needle,
still on the bus, you gazed
out and then it seemed I was Dionysus
and you Diana or another in the bays.
I rushed towards you as if Zeus
heard you when you turned to me, amazed,
and said "It's strange to see the world through
your arm."

Afternoons

it's fine to wake up and hug your knees
my knees
when I have run out of fire fluid
I rush back to bed

the feeling of paws on my knees
petals and wings
little hair
why have you gone

I sing that in my head
being alone is a song
a cigarette in bed
it's better not to touch the ceiling
but if love attaches a band aid
from the ceiling to your head
there's nothing to do but recognize it

And Now to the Stars

A kiss on the glove
At four blows
During lunch I dreamed of mud
But the neck of the waiter
A pink over the blue of the mud
Around your shoes
Was a something
A token I carried
To remember this love was like plastic.

Momentum

I saw the busy street you crossed the last time I saw you
As the river of time, carrying you away forever.
Your pale coat swirled like a leaf in the current
In the crowd of anonymous bodies hurrying back to work.

I turned around and started to walk in the other direction
But because of the tears in my eyes I failed to see a dentist
Standing outside the entrance to his office and collided with him
Knocking him down.

Explanatory Ways

The pain of being a candy bar
in a pub—oh madness it's
beautiful not to be included,
but it's lonely too and makes you remember
the social instincts one can't ever foil!
They're so great! Feeling like a man—what's better than that?

Sunglasses

The air is interesting
My sunglasses today.
Last week they were

Interested by the sea.
In my sunglasses
I look like Grandma Moses

Wearing sunglasses
And interested by the sun,
The air, and the sea.

How hungrily
She looks at the world
Today!

Is it a child's wisdom
In the colorful pine tree
That throws itself upon Grandma Moses?

On her back she fades back
Into the sandy land
And changes slowly to silicates.

How interesting she seems
To my sunglasses
Who cry "Oh Daughter!"

Going to School in France or America

Drugs are a tuition,
and tuition is teaching,
but in French *tuer* is to kill,
and so in France drugs are killing

What does it mean to "make a killing"?
It means to make money,
and money is a means
to certain kinds of killing,

as for instance dropping millions of pennies
on someone from a helicopter.
Money can also be used to buy drugs, helicopters,
or to pay for your tuition,

but money, drugs, and killing
are not the sort of pursuits
a person should pursue with his tuition
if he is a student in France or America

A Crazy American Girl

Pumped for a rhyming line into air
A football falling through registration,
Here I come: That's Kathy's Clown,
A song by Don and Phil in her
Consciousness. And mine. A beverage
Passes between lips, they're her lips;
I am that beverage. Her Royal Crown
Classes break on the hour
Bar, O falcon of the lecture!
Fall, footballs, through the leaves!
We clown in airs of each other's consciousness:
I bring hers stealthy cigarettes,
Between-halves tears; she brings mine
Contemporary milk of the lectures.

Penmanship

If I were Sophocles, brave with truth
I would play my old fiddle a sharp tune or two
And then withdraw into the uniqueness of rock
Which your special penmanship changes into lock
For your l's are special, as in Elgin Penitentiary
Where you have never been, my expressive farmer
Preferring liberty to freedom or a penitentiary

The baroque swoop in your l's is for enhancing liking
I like you because I am mad at you
Often you are mad at me too
All very spectacular
But it's awful when the other person isn't breathing

Friendship tempts you to essay the r in rock while breathing
Your friend Rock likes you
Jean
Frank
Paul
Matthew
Joy
Austin
And people
Like that
Like you
Goya is a tremendous painter

Goya is dead

But the poetry of penmanship is never dead

While you are writing

We survive for a while, and then we die

And this is but the beginning

Your d pirouettes then later you die

But there is no reason for you to care about any of that

For you have become the virtuoso of capital F

Even if tomorrow we die

I am still free to go on choosing whoever I like

I go on choosing you

And you go on choosing me

Over and over again

Irrespective of merit

Superballs

You approach me carrying a book
The instructions you read carry me back beyond birth
To childhood and a courtyard bouncing a ball
The town is silent there is only one recreation
It's throwing the ball against the wall and waiting
To see if it returns
One day
The wall reverses
The ball bounces the other way
Across this barrier into the future
Where it begets occupations names
This is known as the human heart a muscle
A woman adopts it it enters her chest
She falls from a train
The woman rebounds 500 miles back to her childhood
The heart falls from her clothing you retrieve it
Turn it over in your hand the trademark
Gives the name of a noted maker of balls

Elastic flexible yes but this is awful
You say
Her body is limp not plastic
Your heart is missing from it
You replace your heart in your breast and go on your way

I'm on an Island

Do not try to adopt me
I am not a pigmy soothed
Boy or baby hitchhiker saint

What is wrong suddenly
Is that I swallow a cold
Blast of air, I mean fright

Spill coffee on my book
And hear the kinks
In the great universe

The warp in the coffin
Phantom men fly out of
Anywhere in this world

Daily News

Dying day pinches the tot
He grabs my pen and beads
And plays into my hands
His father's skull glistens
Across his wife's white arms

The past bursts on a flower
And softly erases its bulb
We hear this going on all around
Night packs the traffic in cotton
And 1st Ave. fruit stands in opal

It is his first day to hurl a toy
But a grey torch rises in the future
Like a pair of scissors
The dark unravels towards
As I return to my newspaper

Sonnet

Five A.M. on East Fourteenth I'm out to eat
The holiday littered city by my feet a jewel
In the mire of the night waits for the light
Getting and spending and day's taxi cry   The playful

Waves of the East River move toward their date
With eternity down the street, the slate sky
In Tompkins Square Park prepares for the break
Through of lean horses of morning   I

Move through these streets like a lamplighter
Touch ragged faces with laughter by my knowledge
Of tragic color on a pavement at the edge
Of the city   Softly in the deep East River water

Of dreams in which my long hair flows
Slow waves move   Of my beginnings, pauses

The Lake

1

Poets, do not sneer at everything
A tree is like organized crime
It spreads its roots everywhere
When you sing of a tree
You sneer at justice   Goodbye, Lake
Poets! The radio is chinking out
Caprice Espagnole by Lao-Tree

There's not much beauty here
Just a speck, a crumb
That's fallen on your dress
From a table full of ugliness
Look, on this small speck
I will subsist like a coot
In my cornflake nest

2

The horse in the picture
Has two legs raised high   He is
Waving to someone   Probably
A lady horse   You are so beautiful
In my mind because you are not

A horse   The farmer takes a wife
He sits upon her torse
And creates little farmers
And farmeresses   Then he goes out
For a ride on his horse   Lady,
I ride straight to you
Like a line out of a geometry
Book   Madonna! Lady of Mythic
Motions, Lady of Mondrian, Lady of the Lake

3

I like timber art   There's lots
Of it here at the lake
Above the timber there are snows
And above that, a wolf
I write you long letters
From my cabin here by the lake
Where I write late

Long poems and letters
From a lone wolf
Who likes you
And hates art
Like this lake art
The snow creates on my breath
With its wolfish flakes

4

I have several pets
Among them a wolf
And a horse   A legendary lumberjack
Created them for me
With a hoisting apparatus
Whose strong beams
Move deep in the lake

My pet, my legendary dreams
Of you among the lumber
Of this ordinary lake
Are distant as a wolf
And skittish as a horse
But out of them I hoist
You, my love, my pet creation

5

Some disorganized *concerti*
Are skidding across the house
Like a horse skidding
Across the ice on the lake
The arm is far from sturdy
It makes zigzag lines
On the apparatus

No one can cross the snow's arms to
The distant timber
Lines of creation, for beyond
Them nothingness lies
Like a wolf and waits with death
For the horse, and its ordinary
Rider to cross the lake

6

Lake Life, I want to take a bath
In you and forget death
Waits at the muddy bottom
Although I live in the tree
Of poetry and sing, I have no
Water wings
And fear death by drowning

Sometimes I get a pain in my breath
Apparatus, then I stop breathing
Long enough to count the trees
Across the lake, and the leaves
Whirling on the water
Start to sink slowly, in circles
That down deep, become straight lines

Where I Live

The stars flow beneath the water
The clouds freeze or collapse
In laughter, lure like a pledge
Like hockey, trust, language
Approach and spit on a flower
Cruelly and scream in the forest
Of mildness, portrayed by art
As endless steps into the sky
But while all this is going on
An aimed surmise, noiseless
As the heaven that gathers it
Banishes beauty-hemmed man
To bed, as sleep extinguishes
The planet in whirring dreams
Where slowness flows to be
Breathless, like a bicyclist.

"My heart in pieces . . ."

My heart in pieces like the bits
Of traffic lost in the blue
Rain confused I roar off into
To learn how to build a ladder
With air in my lungs again
To be with you in that region
Of speed and altitude where our bodies
Sail off to be kissed and changed
By light that behaves like a hand
Picking us up in one state and putting
Us down in a different one every time

1968–1978

Now She Dwells Here

It was the work of fortune
which brings joy and not pain only.
But can a winged thing become less?

She lived on E. 75th Street
to speak plainly.

I mean: in the divisiveness of love
two people pass through
the same instant separately

for all their awareness sighs
for life and not for each other
but in doing that it does.

Pillow

for Angelica

Our arms sleep
Together under water

Air curves into the room
On feathers

Apple leaf light
Beneath the blankets

A butterfly of hair
In the breeze

One

Light spray over a daisy chain of days.
Many wives, brought on rocking boats,
Dissolve into one loved damsel.
Jury of sighs, it is Time
To load the back with groceries
With my brother and my wife
Because life is a family.
Did I drive right? Risky slopes
Deer start across, hushed timber
Cool and the engine smoking.
When mouths of fog cover the truck
Pushed by wind, the ocean sends
Us violet shrouds, bears
Brush us in the dark eucalyptus.
Where the hawk dives, a flowing zone
Lights the road. A brown head whispers
In the restless advance of trees
And cars, friends of lonesome men
In the brunt of a huge wave.

Nimble Rays of Day
Bring Oxygen to Her Blood

After the sponge bath
Spice cake and coffee
In a sky blue china cup

Tiny clouds float by
Like bits of soap
In a bowl of very blue water

A happy baby sleeps
In a silky chamber
Of my wife's lovely body

A leaf spins itself
The leaf's a roof
Over the trembling flower

Everything's safe there
Because nothing that breathes
Air is alone in the world

Up in Here

All her aroused feelings
    pour through a hole
        changing from particles to waves
      of noise to bury every signal

You chop your way out of the vocal bush
        using your cane for a pool cue
            now the shot
      the word pops into place
    bing!

You are passionate but afraid
        to fuse someone's mood
    the "you" that is asleep
    to the "she" that is you   a model
     of light and logic
       but you do

A pledge of allegiance to the mobility of the day
      where a bird lights on a branch
    like a beautiful song lighting on itself
     to bring you grace

Short Order

Poppy
Sweet pea

                      Bluebell spumoni

On white, please, and a dash of air

Here, too, where the sky is blue

                            Cobalt
                            Lupin

Air

The sweet peas, pale diapers
Of pink and powder blue, are flags
Of a water color republic.
The soft bed, turned back,
Is a dish to bathe in them.
This early in the morning
We are small birds, sweetly lying
In it. We have soft eyes,
Too soft to separate the parts
Of flowers from the water, or
The angels from their garments.

Things About You

1

I write this for your eyes and ears and heart
If it makes your eyes sore
               ears weary
                    and heart burn
                         Stop!

                    I come to things about you
               I didn't use to understand

I didn't mean to use you
                    I just summoned you

Then at the end you are soft and bent
The way a tulip is droopy a lilac is not

                    knowing this
               is a joyous experience
                    for me
          gives you endless pleasure

You are casual when the others are only easy

You go directly toward your own thought

There are some things about you I don't understand
        that's why I married you

Do you think these are banal thoughts?

       that IS what it's all about
           the portrait for instance
   of the *inside* of the surface of something

The way *You Didn't Even Try* is "about"

Do out and in exist?

                   and up and down
                are lies about them

2

Did you say something?

80°

white butterfly

   dancing albino speck

       tiny hanky

    scarfs

      the swiss chard

there in the entero-system I imagine it cool

       Switzerland!

  pale sweet pea snows wild radish lakes

    CABBAGE MOTH

on a day like this your thirst is easy to identify with

at five o'clock eighty degrees of

wild July fire-and-jewel spectrum

humming bird goat bell bluejay feather etc.

but what about the { other } butterflies

      { "real" }

  what about the frogs?

They're back in muddy February

         "in mothballs"

A Perfect Stranger

that 40's character in the fedora
who works in the meaning room
and programmed this September morning
moonlight to be you
                              I don't know him

His name comes over the wire as Panama Red

a carrot top from the Canal Zone

It burns the silver off the wires as it spins

Locations

for Ted Berrigan

Waking up in the time zones
                out of bed
           to the telephone

and down the line
               by instant
         across the Pacific
                    Mountain
               Central

to a tree sized town's
               frozen spaces
        where you sit
        temporarily
                        warm
      in an office
        off a corridor
     of a long brick
       and glass hall

haven
    in the middle of the night
     with your socks
     on the desk's
      manuscripts
      & friendly
       transcontinental voice

*   *   *

     lost at first
I leap on the words
       later the lovely
      impulse inside them
         lights up the way

Hush, Hush

I know these radio waves
are being stored away
in my brain somewhere
even tho I'm not here
to pay any attention
              to them

They'll come back later as
frequency-modulated
variety shows and UHF cabaret

This is what I was thinking, Ted

For instance, while I was
              writing this
the following music
    came into my head:

Overture to *Sonata for Trumpets & Strings*
              By Henry Purcell
Miles Davis: *Ssh . . . Peaceful*
Jimmy Reed: *Hush, Hush*

Slow Life

1

Cinematic blossoming of love gasoline

2

Blue windows behind the stars
      and silver flashes moving across them
    like spotlights at movie premieres

  long cool windshield wiper bars

3

the butterfly gently opens itself like a fist
      dividing into wings   and drifting off
          over the cube's puzzled head

August 6, 1969

A moon in the blue morning
Like a high fly to the outfield
In Gemini Stadium
Meadow garden atmosphere sky pill
Cactus flower on fire in the green
I fall on the belly of life I bleat
Can't tell why Little Milton feels so bad

Magic Arrival No. 7

Not less because in purple I descend
The western day through what you called
The loneliest air did you arrive at what you are,
A unison of every fragrant thing yet brief
Like the perfection, after rain, of the color
Blue, its clear articulation in the air
When it and the sun suddenly come in the room together

Crows

Like the shore's alternation of door   wave
Shoe   wave, the displaced and disturbed
Air replaces itself with more air as casually
As attention grants itself, and I observe
Two crows sew themselves onto the lace flag
Of that flying cloud, whose cosmetic grace
Adorning the Plain Jane face of the day
Pins them in an unlikely halo of pale light
After one blast of which they dance away,
Croaking shrilly as abandoned divas
Whose black scarves flap in the breeze
Over every home and panorama, dark precise
Signs washed up on the air to be noticed
Out of a continuous process of succession

Back to the Front

A breeze blowing between the worlds
   air here and the heavenly ones

Nearly knocks my head off
                    on my front lawn

Where everything aspires to be sky
with delicate green arms

               That's what I want to do
go away on the light feet of my thoughts

            Back inside where nothing's palpable
As far away from here as possible

The Tire

The story thread runs out through your hands
To many places, indicating them as snags.
You take the tire apart. Even so, the process
Solves its own knots as it continues—gingerly—
To slip out of your hands. There is always
A looseness, open and moving, it says here
In the event. Then why does every tug on the
Strings complicate everything, ravelling
Up further the almost impossible ball? When
Know-how shows itself for what it is, will Grace
Grow free and exact to award the useless
Virtues their place? Do I have to wrestle
With every thought on earth like this? I mean
Will an angel arrive and untangle them all?

Eos

Solar emeralds melt and blend
In a slow flash flow
Silver eucalyptus sails above
Waves of lavender
We rise at daybreak
Light opens its pure brooch
Far out over the ocean
A machine of perfect touch

Sky

The green world thinks the sun
Into one flower, then outraces
It to the sea in sunken pipes.
But twisting in sleep to poetry
The blood pumps its flares out
Of earth and scatters them. And
They become, when they shine on
Beauty to honor her, a part of
Her laconic azure, her façade.

The Greeks

Deep in the air the past appears
As unreal as air to the boy
Or the apple of the world
To a girl whose eyes are pale and mild
Her hair is probably not real gold
Only a good imitation of the Greeks'
Like a map of that world of early days
Where woman lives on a scarlet cloud
While man in colorless blunt noon
Splashes up at the blue variables
That pass by on an airplane of words
Into the sky which distributes gifts of
Rain and light over our lives equally
Infinite gifts we are unable to behold

The Byrds

"... a magic carpet ride"

We are saturated by and
absorbed in the fluent
circuits of this energy

It snakes through you to be a
star in nova—all stored
force of the cosmos pours

Down the dorsal rosary
in phosphor flow, like
spinning discs in flicker—

Continuity, power, peace.
So in space ease seals me,
accepts me, I am released.

Bugs Ate This Lake Clean

Conversation
words = canned reasoning

Grammar tells us
what kind of an object
anything is. So does light.

Chapeau Electrique

He has turned
his hat on.

What do you turn on
when you turn on?

It rips them off
of energy
to come on angry
at somebody

"Thought
 is surrounded
 by a
 halo . . ."

You can feel yourself thinking
but can you think yourself feeling?

A state of what?

"You're a smarty pants
do you want to dance?"

CONCEPTS ARE INSTRUMENTS

Cigarettes are like women.
The best ones are thin and rich.

"A lot of Women's Liberation people object
very strongly to that song," says the disc
jockey, after playing "Just Like a Woman"—
"but it's a real situation just the same."

Casino Royale

"Think of me as the second woman in
your life—the one after Mata Hari."

My wife and my daughter
lying in bed with me
talking about money
(Bolinas 1970)

Don't let the light go out till
I can let all I hold to go

Touch is important
in a dark universe,
but print is useless
much less unreal.

The Singing Cells
The Night of the Living Dead

MEAT SILENCE

All things pass
And so do the places they pass through

Any resistance
is no good

Mechanical Tao

The robot pushes small obstacles out of the
way, goes round heavy ones, and avoids slopes.

To slide around those corners on
Mount Tamalpais with—Volvo ad

NO THINKING
    (9.17.70)

The BIG crayon
for little fingers

Where is it written
that we must write
right side up?

Advantage—
ah, it stays with us
past the asking

Are we
some kind
of filter, some
diode

it's all being
run through?

I am here with this (my mind, etc.)
"I am not here with my mind"

Being
is dying
by loving

To live in the world as it is
& save your soul too
is a lot to do

Learning to forget
occurring in the instant,
uneasily wise
& so, poorly aware

Space isn't
in Language—
or as Juliet cries
"Outside! Outside!"

I walk in
on occasion

One room fronts on
open, unqualified spaces.
The other is bound
by a wall. All its
area is thought up.

mind
lines

The Everly Bros—
all their songs
are like dreams

I dig mountains
to look at.
Ocean,
be by.

KARMA ARMS

where the stars stay
when they're in town

Angels carry messages—
like DNA?

Juliet swings past
in ski pants
for the love of Krishna

Happier than I thought I was

"What has the greatest importance
is not the twelve tones, but,
much more, the serial conception . . ."

MORE
More hair
every
day

Lively,
the voices
move.
A lovely,
roving
mind.

Wife,
friend
for life
if ever.

The music—
go with it—

as, bathed,
one floats.

Bugs ate this lake clean.

Paper People

Polite people of the future
I see you wearing paper dresses
Living in paper houses
And flying on paper planes

I hope you know how to read this

Nouns

Around
nouns
people are
nervous,
possessive.

Nothing Inside

People on television
give you their
public self

like people
on elevators

Things to Watch Out For in California

1. Inertia
2. Highway Patrol

Brainards

Joe's red poppies
on black
have presence

and when I look
at them I know
presence is energy

on a cool surface
a big hot process
inside steady eyes

Novel

memory
sleep
genius
hypnotism
fatigue
lunacy

Heavy

When the gods die
the myths
are lifted off our backs.

Peace be with them.
They were heavy.

from SMACK

Because
the asking
of original
questions
is a
consequence
of
interferences
and because
interferences
are products
of
time sequences
it follows
that original
questions
are both
functions
and products
of
time.

*

All
the great
ideologies
of the
world
are
predicated
on Malthus'
assumption
that
there is
not
enough
to sustain
both
you
and me.

*

If
you play
James
Brown's
"Money
Won't
Change

You"
in a
bank
the total
environment
is changed.

*

The only
people
who will
escape
will be
those
who have
the
seal
of God
on their
foreheads.

*

The bitter
and

frustrated
residual
feeling
due to
a lousy
shtup
afflicts
millions more
Americans
than does
halitosis.

*

It
is not
surprising
that faced
with
universal
destruction
our art
should
at last
speak
with unimpeded
force

and unveiled
honesty
to a future
which
may well
be non-existent
in
a last
effort
of recognition
which
is the
justification
of
being.

*

Applied
to the
brain
we find
that this
device
which is
about
the size

and shape
of a
beer bottle
can
penetrate
the neural
noise
and gossip
so that
we can
detect
and recognize
the specific
or general
response
to our
sensory
interrogation
at levels
of signal
that
we never
dreamed
of before.

*

The mammals
give off
the gases
that are
necessary
to
the survival
of
the vegetation
while
the vegetation
gives off
the gases
that are
necessary
to
the survival
of
the mammals.

*

The orders
given
the machine
are fed
into it

91

by
a taping
which is
completely
predetermined
but
the actual
contingencies
met
in the
performance
of the
machine
are handed
over
as
a basis
of
further regulation
to
a new
control tape
constructed
by
the machine
itself.

33 Statements

Rothko's hovering tiers of atmospheric color attack Keokuk, Iowa.
Johns's tonic simplicity of stripes and circles is in some ways a cop-out.
De Kooning, Pollock and Kline's athletic calligraphy derives from surfing.

Stella's monastic designs appeal to lemurs.
Mondrian's black bars on white grounds rise and shine.
Newman's variations on an ostensibly straight line are in fact crooked.

Ad Reinhardt's black paintings were left out in the rain overnight.
Manet's qualities of absence cause skin disease.
Andy Warhol's rows of ten-by-twenty cans don't contain Campbell's soup.

Kenneth Noland's target, chevron and stripe paintings mime the
    noodling movements of antique biplanes.
Donald Judd and Robert Morris's stubbornly indivisible equal-unit
    designs suck.
Johns's sculpmetal embalmments of a light bulb and a flash light emit a
    glow of total friendliness.

Monet's chromatic and luminary variations on such themes as a haystack
    look OK.
Frank Stella's pictures of "nothing" are just that.
Roy Lichtenstein's Pop paintings bubble upwards.

Le Corbusier's 1939 plan for an infinitely expandable museum went down
    the toilet.
Malevich and Mondrian's conceptual idealism threw us off the track.

Judd and Morris's antagonism to marks of personal handicraft is like God's.

Mondrian and Newman's Eureka quality of beauty fails completely.
Stella's art turns me on.
Jasper's Dilemma is the state motto of Utah.

Mondrian's tough irreducible nut of radiant energy indicates drug abuse.
Stella's enclosed field of multiple unfocused activities shows that he is a secret jackoff artist.
Kenneth Noland's chevron paintings of 1963-64 were commissioned by an insect.

Jasper Johns's "0-9" lithographs of 1963 tell us to make love not war.
Miriam Schapiro, Larry Zox, Ron Davis and Darby Bannard's investigation of fictive depth on a plane surface would be possible only under capitalism.
Pollock and Kline's participation in a field of forces is old hat.

Morris Louis and Kenneth Noland's searing antibodies of color make whoopee.
Robert and Sonia Delaunay's rainbow disks smack of homework.
Newman's thin bands on open fields of color decorate Uranus.

Roy Lichtenstein's parodies of the aggressively "moderne" fooled the police.
Darby Bannard's curious pastel blandness relates to a hatred of arithmetic.
De Kooning's impact is not to be spoken of here.

Safari

Thoughts in
shorthand

head in
the clouds

that tone
goes on & on

when it ends
it's gone

"clear as a
bell"

the ocean's
motion

the cat's meow

the phone rings
in the Sahara

the sky is blue
there is no one to talk to

Imagine

9/22: Blue sky w/ tiny white clouds. Painted the house white.

Big white pianos. John Lennon.

Granular. Pearly. You got the silver. "I got the agate."
(A milky grey *inside* the white).

Tonality. "The Blue-Grey Game."

Sand.
Vanilla.
Light.

Snowy keys.

"The whites of their eyes." Ivory walls. Blank paper.

White Coffee. Lace Noise. Cocaine. Negatives.

Air. An absence of color, between beige & azure.

Dice, bones & teeth. *Blue Angel.* Ariel (Ono).

Moon Rock Survey. Sugar Bowl Blues. French windows.

Frosted Oars.

Whistle Buoy

That grey droning note
  I've heard every dusk

Neither owl nor foghorn
  but similar to both

The low fluted "day-is-done"
  of some unknown warbler

Atonally breathy memo
  of universal mysterioso

Tucks misty roses away
  in the dark's soft envelope

Safe under a lion's paw
  of starry numerology

Whose silver figures
  fleck the surf's Afro

Otherwise sparkling brassily
  into the liquid air

Life Notes

Like a big tired buffalo
                    or ox
Mount Tam kneels beneath
                    a glittering ceiling
her blue and green
                    flanks rest, her shaggy
head settles
                    and drinks from the lagoon.
The fur of her underbelly is burnt and brown
cars wind down it
                    like ticks. The top
of her head is yellow and balding
except where a few squiggly redwood tips
crest it. She rests, in the blazing
light of a June afternoon, as I do.

Life is not conditional. IF
is only a
            half-life.
A Whole Life—yours, mine, its—
can pass by in an instant. Hers
continues, like a music without notes,
unless you really strain
your ears to hear them, and maybe even then.

Ah—There

the emerald mosque
    in motion
        every time a fern

touches
    the honey
        colored comb

she pulls
    through her
        fallen hair

The Door to the Forest

for Jim Carroll

Eric Dolphy can't wake up:
the green light's still burning
by the gate. Pine cones

when stepped on by
dogs or raccoons, click
gently, like bones

into the mist, which
smells like mint; the
sounds diminish it;

the white fire rose
through the dropper's eye
falls; and the rain remains.

Hot Dog

I am watching Mouse Factory with one eye
and my other eye is on Warren Jabali
who steals the ball and drives bravely
and at half time a returning POW (black)
admits he'd like a piece of the pie
but they'll probably be giving lumpy gravy
laced with the snow white pacifier
that'd keep even King Kong in line
the Greeks gave it credit for wonders of nature
which by the way applies to this here Julius Erving
who lopes in for a backward slam while I blink
then glides upcourt like a Clipper Ship

Poetry Street

On Poverty Street, the disinterested
click of Dixie Cups on bakelite trays
reminds me that prose exists.

Campaign

The Nix surfboards along on the
electronic wave as triumphantly as
ol' Hitler rode the mechanical wave of voodoo . . .

one thing's for sure. It's pain in the hair time again
for America's walking weird
and the dancing robots are going to be front & center.

9/25/72

Evolution

Virtually headlong
  into the smoothly breaking day
  the whole organism surged
   so that nothingness was
    but a small blurt upon the All:

Eternity bathed this instant in
                silent Gold.

Then, inexorably,
    as into the Valley of Death
     rode the Ten Thousand,
       came the curiosity seekers.

On Venus

I like breathing better than work
but strange is the meat
when it is yanked out of the sky
and arrows are shot into it
Nothing is personal then
and everything is true
including both love's great circumambience
and the hideous skull-glare in the mirror
which pulses and glows
like some videotape of the future

Water

The fog comes in, flatter
than ever. The air, apparently

is blue somewhere, not here.
Flat and linear. The women

can't escape except through speech
so they go to the beach.

I know. I'll talk to
the wall and for once, tell all.

I'll be its friend
as it bends, and fall with it.

One More Saturday Night

Through the night
It snows on the
Sierras as it does
On the grave of
Apollinaire in the
Cemetery of Père
Lachaise
             and on
The radio I get
Truck music from
San Jose:
"Want to make it to
Amarillo by
Morning . . ."
                    "just
Because you ask me to."

The green oak
Burns weakly
In the grate
And as I write
In the window
Of the loft
The light
Turns blue.

The Stars

No one sees the insane shining
Spaces where the stars pass
Time by drowning their aloneness
In the high of the truly deep

Breadwinning

The Hound of the Basketball summons me
With a sort of scarlet thud
As blood passeth before my eyes
And I realize it's time to arise and go
To the school
To shoot a few hoops
In the saffron air of twilight

I drive in for a layup worth 50¢
Reminding me that
My agenda still includes
The acquisition of bank notes
Sufficient unto the purchase of foodstuffs
And transportation of the items so obtained

What Wordsworth called "getting and spending"
Meaning to pass money through space
In a circulatory repetition I find tedious
Though it does have a tautological beauty
Like the reincarnation of victims in cartoons

It's odd to live on a rubber band like that
So off I go to the post office
And send mss. to New York
Whence grammar tries to force itself on me
And bend me into a spectator of life

But I run off down Mesa Road to the silver tanks
Punching the air and hollering things
Piltdown Man would understand

And on my way
I am leapt upon by a slavering collie
Whom I beat back with blows of a rolled up shirt
Much as in time of crisis one harks back
To Australopithecus
For when grunts proceed from this form divine
And drool at the corner of its mouth rudely gathers
Then may one perceive its actual origins
And the bush-browsing Homo Erectus is recollected

So I get on the mental trolley and ride homeward
Wondering if
Any more chores remain
Like large holes
In the side of the Trojan Horse jello mold?

The words are massed there
Deeper than my probes may go
Though I have given them
A Frankensteinian energy
Still I am not surgeon of happy tunes that shake the walls
So I must chop through the mush
To where the earthlings are waiting to be fed
And put to bed

They receive the package of hot dogs with happy chirps
And day is done
And this is good
For now I have permission
To fuck off

Baseball & Classicism

Every day I peruse the box scores for hours
Sometimes I wonder why I do it
Since I am not going to take a test on it
And no one is going to give me money

The pleasure's something like that of codes
Of deciphering an ancient alphabet say
So as brightly to picturize Eurydice
In the Elysian Fields on her perfect day

The day she went 5 for 5 against Vic Raschi

Radio

Don't hurt the radio for
Against all
Solid testimony machines
Have feelings
Too

Brush past it lightly
With a fine regard
For allowing its molecules
To remain 100% intact

Machines can think like Wittgenstein
And the radio's a machine
Thinking softly to itself
Of the Midnight Flower
As her tawny parts unfold

In slow motion the boat
Rocks on the ocean
As her tawny parts unfold

The radio does something mental
To itself singingly
As her tawny parts unfold
Inside its wires
And steal away its heart

Two minutes after eleven
The color dream communicates itself
The ink falls on the paper as if magically
The scalp falls away
A pain is felt
Deep in the radio

I take out my larynx and put it on the blue chair
And do my dance for the radio
It's my dance in which I kneel in front of the radio
And while remaining motionless elsewise
Force my eyeballs to come as close together as possible
While uttering a horrible and foreign word
Which I cannot repeat to you without now removing my larynx
And placing it on the blue chair

The blue chair isn't here
So I can't do that trick at the present time

The radio is thinking a few licks of its own
Pianistic thoughts attuned to tomorrow's grammar
Beautiful spas of seltzery coition
Plucked notes like sandpaper attacked by Woody Woodpecker

The radio says Edwardian farmers from Minnesota march on the Mafia
Armed with millions of radioactive poker chips

The radio fears foul play
It turns impersonal
A piggy bank was smashed
A victim was found naked
Radio how can you tell me this
In such a chipper tone

Your structure of voices is a friend
The best kind
The kind one can turn on or off
Whenever one wants to
But that is wrong I know
For you *will intensely* to *continue*
And in a deeper way
You do

Hours go by
And I watch you
As you diligently apply
A series of audible frequencies
To tiny receptors
Located inside my cranium
Resulting in much pleasure for someone
Who looks like me
Although he is seated about two inches to my left
And the both of us
Are listening to your every word
With a weird misapprehension
It's the last of the tenth

And Harmon Killibrew is up
With a man aboard

He blasts a game winning home run
The 559th of his career
But no one cares
Because the broadcast is studio-monitored for taping
To be replayed in 212 years

Heaven must be like this, radio
To not care about anything
Because it's all being taped for replay much later

Heaven must be like this
For as her tawny parts unfold
The small lights swim roseate
As if of sepals were the tarp made
As it is invisibly unrolled
And sundown gasps its old Ray Charles 45 of "Georgia"
Only through your voice

Nine Songs

College Music

Students walk back and forth
Between large, squarish buildings,
Carrying their books.

Airplane Music

The plastic trays on the
Laps of the passengers
Jiggle up and down.

TV Music

At 3 A.M., television tells
its secrets to the
armchair sleeper.

Sex Music

Wiry pubic hairs
scratch against each other
deep in the condominium.

Baseball Music

A hot dog paper blows across
the infield, passing into
shadows near third base.

Office Music

The hanged man's voice
emerges from the dress
of the secretary.

Hospital Music

At night the noises of
those breathing
make a difficult muzak.

Bar Music

He tilts his head
back, and pours his
drink into it.

Highway Music

The cars go by
just like they did
yesterday.

from SUITE

Got to be there, so that she'll know
when she's with me she's home. On
the air waves across the nation
energy imagines it can move that way.
But sleep hides her modes as nature's.
Her skin is a dreaming surface—
blood drifts up through shadows,
light shifts on minimal rubies,
the spots on water where fish breathe . . .
impossible to see them coldly
or in some numerical epitome.

What the picture tells me is itself.
Now I know how to go on:
hold still, dry your eyes.
Life is actual, warm and near
and completely without character
except for the melodious enigma
of her body and the possibility
of monkeying around with it quite soon.
Otherwise, the room contains only
a metal writing table, a chair,
a flower box, and *The Corpse* of Balthus.

The tones of voice are petty
for a while, then change to affection
then quiet is disclosed like
a jaguar running on damp grass
and the heartfalls converge for an
instant at speechless thunder now.
Neither knows whose limbs are whose,
or whether they are those of automata.
For a moment the ocean reaches in the window
and painlessly strangles consciousness
with a sheer cloth—a pair of ladies' hose?

Her voice is heard, and then the child's
who is her daughter, and they both sound
very young, they are both young girls
and they are talking in the garden
under the pear trellis, and their
hair shines in the sun, and the pear
petals snow on them, and they are one
person, going down through linear
time, but apart from it, parallel
and talking, and breathing again
and flashing and moving along that line

Warm ripe days. The sun floods the ridge with color
before dawn, slowly the reddish light implodes
and before dusk the moon floats up like a softball

over the ocean. Starbright glimmers the weather
satellite in a position akin to that of Venus
or is it the skylab people coming down? Mutual
interests unite people on earth and in the sky,
ah and the heart sighs to be so satisfied
it beats against the skin to bespeak love's beauty
and the air brushes past it with a smoothness
borne by zephyrs from somewhere far inland
where the days are hard but the nights are long and warm
from various small fires static electricity causes
to crackle in the sheets, and draw up our auras.

And Don't Ever Forget It

Take off that apron
And put your red dress on
No
On second thought
Take off that red dress
And lay back
On my big brass bed
In your pink slip
The one with flowers sewn on it
Not the one
That certifies the registration of your auto

It's a lovely auto
I just don't like it
Because it has kudzu vines
Growing out of its body
And you know how I hate kudzu vines

I Was Born to Speak Your Name

I knew the tune
It was my song
Even before you came along
Yet only then did I perceive its meaning

This *you* I wished for
This desired Other of whom
I spoke so glowingly in poems
I never knew its name

When I lifted its arms up
I noticed tiny wings
That's all I knew
The rest was Muselike
Anonymous this "you"

So I guess those poems
Were like phonecalls to the future
I think I had your number
Knew what I was looking for
Even before I found it
In the face directory

And luckiest of all
Your human substance
Was life's loveliest
Far as I could see

As if I'd placed
Bones and skin
Together in a dream
You were put together that way
But I wouldn't let it go to my head if I were you

Every Day

Awake the mind's hopeless so
At a quarter to six I rise
And run 2 or 3 miles in
The pristine air of a dark
And windy winter morning
With a light rain falling
And no sound but the pad
Of my sneakers on the asphalt
And the calls of the owls in
The cypress trees on Mesa Road

And when I get back you're
Still asleep under the warm covers
Because love is here to stay
It's another day and we're both still alive

Gift of Tongue

It's Christmas Eve and I run in the sun
There's not much holiday traffic on Mesa

A VW goes by with surf board sticking
Up through the roof like a shark fin
A girl on a black horse says "Hi!"

Christmas trees line the center of Brighton
Kids went to the city and got em
One of em's even covered with real snow

So goodbye to another year and I don't know
What to make of it though I'm fairly
Sure it won't be money
I'm pondering that seriously

When you come down the stairs in blue velvet
Like a long cool drink of water viewed
Through a prism of purest ultramarine
And all of a sudden I can speak English

Jan. 8

Large yellow full moon
Sets over my shoulder
As I run home from Palo
Marin in the pre-dawn coldness
Blowing small white
Airpuffs out ahead of me

On my right the ocean shines
Like hot asphalt
Moment of inky mystery
And mirage!

                  Then in the east a Rose
Of Sharon saffron-ness sweeps
Over Mount Tam whose
Sleeping volumes are still
Snow-dusted

                And slowly
Overhead the whole bowl
Of sky brightens and expands
Counter-clockwise

Birds

Sky full of blue nothing toward which the Magi
Move, like dream people who are Walt Fraziers of the air . . .
Sometimes the moves they make amaze them
For they will never happen again, until the end of time; but there they are.

So shall I be like them? I don't think so . . . and yet to float
Above the rolling H_2O
On wings that express the mechanics of heaven
Like a beautiful golden monkey wrench
Expresses mechanics of earth . . . t'would be bueno.

Euphrates River

Morning beckons from the phthalocyanine shade
Heaviness sheds its weight
There's water everywhere even in the Arno

Unrivaled dawns and dusks so wild
Yet most sensational of all is Eve
Her hands like leaves
Move chastely in the air
And many little cries—according to Alberti—
Come out of the branches
Near by, whispering *foglie* . . .

The wax paper crackles around the sandwich
In Botticelli's hands
As he relaxes beside his canvas
Having lunch

He dreams of white feet
In sweaty little ballet slippers
Ahhh . . .

His heart is stoked
With the pale fire that
Burnt Siena

A New Light

The sandpapery candor of Bobby Dylan
Strikes a jejune note all of a sudden

Throw my ticket out the window
Throw my sneakers out there too

Mama said there'd be days like this
When rain pencils the sky

With an air of biological rigor
And visibility is grimly minimized

Tiny puffs of smoke speckle it
The harmonic spectrum is muffled

The tall white dog stands in the road
Shivering and shaking the water off

The scene makes the usefulness
Of an infinite tolerance evident

Too late I see the value of being
Resolute in a new light

Gale

At forty unusual phenomena occur. The chimney
    whistles & the windows blister (rain).
At fifty to sixty it chases the cat in, breaks the
    pinebranch (Bishop), rips the eucalyptus leaf
    loose, wakes the baby, shakes the roof & bangs
    the door.
At seventy individual sounds subside in the general roar.
At eighty a flash heralds the arrival of Storm King
    in a black leather riding outfit (Coldwater Canyon,
    1941), accompanied by Mildred Pierce, stunning
    in a mauve chemise by de Kooning. Everybody's drunk
    flooded puddle in the bloody rain and driving
At this point transmission ended due to power failure.

Winter Storm on Alder Road

It rains endlessly and the ocean wind blows a blue light in from
    the south
A blue cloud broken into arms like a tree and dark
And a spark
Of life glimmers in me
As I climb up to the roof
Spooning blacktar into the cracks in the moulding
The wind blowing buckets of rain back in my face
Me screaming my tar song into the rain
The rain screaming its wet song back at me
When suddenly
I grasp the problem of life

Is it possible to live so that life stops being problematic?

I don't grasp the mechanics

The louder I yell the louder the wind gets
And as I slap the black caulking
Onto the window moulding
I see my own reflection
In the window
Shrieking
Back at myself

My hood scares me

From the black sky pours
A hierarchy of drops
Particular objects fly around in the wind

And turning my head to look away from the wind
I see a vision of all life holds in store
Slowly moving toward me

The dusky ape people we move among
And their chattel
Drifting like mobile bumps forever
Beneath the ever reaching rain on the spongy horizon
Across the flooded mesa

They are my lookalikes
These Bolinasian Cro-Magnons

Turning back to my work
I crow
Meaningless words
Out into the Open wound
Of the sky
And
The rain streams down my face anyway

You call that life? the problem of life asks me
Yes! I scream back
And so do my people!

Realism

The smashed weirdness of the raving cadenzas of God
Takes over all of a sudden
In our time. It speaks through the voices of talk show moderators.

It tells us in a ringing anthem, like heavenly hosts uplifted,
That the rhapsody of the pastoral is out to lunch.
We can take it from there.

We can take it to Easy Street.
But when things get tough on Easy Street
What then? Is it time for realism?

And who are these guys on the bus
Who glide in golden hats past us
On their way to Kansas City?

October

The rain falls like dirty string
on the tomb
of the human race

The girl with the red scarf
and the sassy face throws
her flowers on the wet leaves

Her name is Marie
I met her last Tuesday
on the Metro

You know how it is in springtime
A man just can't say no
especially when he is sitting in the seat

reserved for those who have been mutilated in the war

The Big Cigars

It's both never and always a work day for me
I work every day and never get paid
This and putting my pants on one leg at a time
Are two things I have in common with the great geniuses
Einstein, Socrates, Rimbaud
The real heavies of the universe, the big cigars

So Long

Life with its heart down on its hands and knees
Has wasted so much time and lost
90% of the big ones for so long it's not
Worth it, no, I don't care what you say
                          said the champion

35

"The fucking enemy shows up"
—TED BERRIGAN

Sometimes I feel like
I know this thing I need
to tell you all
but you won't listen

Those twenty-two nights
I yelled Venusian songs
into the refrigerator
weren't worth it

At night my head
swells up in dreams
and rolls noiselessly
over the earth

Hot Agate

A shower of gold on the wave
Wings make
A black hole
Opens in the sky
And clarity comes through
Like water from a hose
Call it daybreak

Nothing but billboards of presence
From which the angels' cortege begins
To ascend the fiery stairs

You remember them
Those same flowery stairs
You proved false
When your shoes caught on fire
As you were walking up them

Life Flowed Between Us

Life flowed between us.

It was the voice in the shadows
that flows between the centuries

like dark hair flows
across a pillow.

When I looked,
I knew what it was like
to dip a foot
into the river of forgetfulness.

And the voice said: go ahead.

The Great One

So long Roberto Clemente
you have joined the immortals
who've been bodysnatched
by the Bermuda Triangle

When your plane went down
it forced tears out of grown men
all over the hemisphere
Al Oliver and
even Willie Stargell cried

You had a quiet
pissed-off pride
that made your countrymen
look up to you
even if you weren't
taller than they are

No matter how many times
Manny Sanguillen
dove for your body
the sun kept going down
on his inability to find it

I just hope those Martians realize
they are claiming the rights to
far and away the greatest rightfielder
of all time

Clemente (1934–1972)

won't forget
his nervous
habit of
rearing his
head back
on his neck
like a
proud horse

To Ungaretti

On high the fables blaze.

Giusep', you knew the hard
    Egyptian stars
        twenty years
      before you ever set foot
        on the factual shore
               of that land whose modern poetry
           you were to become
              the father of, Italy

And similarly
    your I
          is grave and slow
    and your longing gains
           on what it longs for
        deliberately
      like a quarter horse, strong
           but not swift,
        taking the thoroughbreds on
          at ten furlongs

You lasted

When you were old and silvery
        you gave Ed Sanders some of your pubic hair

to deal to trivia speculators
to help pay the costs
of his magazine of poetry
proving that
you are more modern than Montale

When I think about you now
I always remember that
under the Southern Cross's wild conflagration
your father
helped build
the Suez Canal

The Last Poem (after Robert Desnos)

I've dreamed so much of you
Walked so much
Talked so much made love to your shadow
So much that there's nothing left of you
What is left
Of me is a shadow
Among shadows but 100
Times more shadowy than the rest
A shadow that will come
To rest
In your life in which the sun
Is so much.

Love (after La Rochefoucauld)

Like ghosts,
  much talked about,
    seldom seen.

The Color of Stepped On Gum

is the color of our times.
The light of our times is
the light in the 14th St.
subway at 2 A.M. The air
of our times is the air of the
Greyhound depot, Market
& Sixth. It is prime time. A passed
out sailor sits pitched
forward like a sack of laundry
in a plastic bucket seat
his forehead resting on
the movie of the week. *The Long Goodbye.*

Crisis on the Savannah

"I must complain the cards are ill-shuffled till I have a good hand."
—JONATHAN SWIFT

"Believing something will happen
   Because I don't want it to
And that some other thing won't
   Because I do"—I wailed to the dealer—

"This is desperation." "Yeah?" he said. But then by
   Your graceful lines, your lioness' mane,
Your heat as you returned from
   Your day in the jungle, you relieved me from

What in myself was desperate,
   What even now insists on wishing
And believing. Still in the sheen of finely-breathing
   Blond hair that covers you,

By the flashing way you move from tree
   To tree, and from room to room,
Making it a bright full house,
   I find at least the light to see the cards I am dealt.

Moving Out

Ten years is a long time. They thought of that,
Then they loaded the furniture on. The sky
Disappeared under iron. They said
Their separate goodbyes to the flowers
And the trees, then they drove away.
Behind them, the place dissolved
Into memories and palpable otherness
But they left in it something that might stay,
The years they had spent making a life
They could not carry away with them, leaving,
But that the house could hold, a residual trace,
For as long as it continued to stand in that place.

1978–1987

Mountain Men

Names like Conger, Bridger, Rollins, Meeker, Berthoud
Echo through these canyons
Like summer thunder, proud and bold.
John Quincy Adams Rollins
Built the first wagon road through
The Great Divide. What didn't Sam Conger do?
A mile from here, you can call his name
And hear your voice return
Twelve times from the deepest shaft
Of the Conger mine. And you know Jim Bridger.

Men of ruthless ego all. But what of the mountain ladies?
Didn't they too have pride? And what about
The narrowing ache in the bed beside
You when she wakes to a rough face
That spells out one hundred years of unpleasant history?

Boulder

These neat little western business boys
        in the button down shirts
            they were born in
               no wrinkles, no creases

It's the New West
            the one where
      the biggest baddest outfit
                    in town
      is something called
          Storage Technology

The Light of the World at 9000 Feet

A big
bossy crested
blue jay
with electric black

wings
and a simonized
gorgeousness
about him

flashes into
the aspens
like sheet
lightning

War

The desert moves like a museum made of light.
Its mighty magnitude goes on and on.
It blasts the sleeping woman in her bed. It
Blasts the sleeping man. They are made clean.
Then the wind moves off to Afghanistan.

These are millennial figures.
The tank sits upon the white sand.
The men are away from home for the first time.
Beyond them the great lonely peaks glisten.
They will hear familiar songs in the night wind.

Over to the east the great fires will burn
And burn. Something moves restlessly along the sand.
The wind picks it up and blows it away over the desert.

It is gone into another dimension.
It is like a memory or an artifact in a museum.
The desert washes everything clean.
A bright dog runs from Kabul to Albuquerque.

A Trip to Erie and Hygiene

When the Chinook comes again in January and
Blows the ice floes off Baseline and Arapahoe
I ride the tract flats of the East trying to understand
The long slide show of history now almost through.

From this hill you can see the blinking signal of the laser
Weapons plant in Platteville. Rocky Flats' stacks are visible.
The whole front range is perpendicular
Reality from here. Beneath this blinding wall

And still in waiting for the holy
Fire to consume it, a three hundred mile long
Strip of prairie unravels slowly
And without intermission from Pueblo to Wyoming.

But why direct too hard a light so late upon
This long frozen dormitory hell
When the wind that moves across these plains like a great lion
Will soon be all that remains of the Blue Hotel?

No Tears for Buccaneers

On a calm sea everybody is a pilot
But this night when the waves bucked like mustangs
The young lady returned to her quarters
Where the shadows turned out to be pirates

No longer wonder at the cruelty of pirates, girl
Men may be read, as well as books, too much
Even we pirates, fascinating as we are,
Have a way of leaving you lonely nights

Thus spoke the dashing Mr. Kidd despite the weather
As a wind rushed in pre-emptively from outer space
It made Runaround Sue wonder about the universe
But the big ship plunged on into the night

A Missing Child

Once the articulation blurs there is only
The excellent romance of the disappointment left,
And the momentum of the mind toward any anomaly,
Any way not to obsess too much about death.

There is also the awful rowing toward infinity
In which the oars become locked
In Great Bear Lake. The snow flies
Blue and icy and fleur de lis-like.

In the cemetery up the road Tom Horn's ghost
And everything else observes the quiet of the dead,
And naturally, too, the mornings grow quite cold
Ever since the sun finally departed.

A light snow fell in the night on Florida.
Mrs. Reynolds looked hard but could not find Deborah.

Secrets of the Estate

Death may be the side of life's mansion
That's always been turned away from us—
But that hasn't kept us, now and then,
From sneaking around to the other side,
Where tall weeds grow over the broken statues,
And peeking in the windows.

After the Slide

After the Flagstaff slide
Grass grows up out of broken
Asphalt like brush strokes by Memling
When the wind blows this strong
The emeralds shift positions on the trees
The great trees bow in the air
The brilliant horizontal light
Catches the bending branches from underneath
Breathes their bright greens
Into the blue violent air
And in this same moment
From behind the first snowy peaks
There comes a kind of
Groaning noise like that of something large awakening

They say places sometimes speak to you most deeply
Just when you are about to leave them

Following Rivers into the Night

for Ed Dorn

I guess it's because
the only things left in this West
I can have any real
respect for
are beauty of character
and beauty of nature

and you know the two
breed one another
in those long miles where
there is nothing to do
as the sun goes down
over the flat horizon
but watch it slowly gild
the surfaces of rivers
from the Belle Fourche
(or Foosh, as the locals say)
to the Cimarron
which will push on into
the darkness with its light
flickering over them like a skin.

Population Control in Gillette

The coal trains go through all night long
with a racket like all of hell being unleashed as noise.
At first, as you lie in bed in your motel room or mobile home
it merely disrupts your sleep, your nervous system. Later you kill
    your dog and wife.

Wyoming

Perhaps it's because it's such a threatening space
what with its great expanse of unaffectionate sky
that workers in this boom region travel from
job to job with their housing intact
& never further than ten feet behind them.

"All I want to do . . ."

All I want to do
is to go
back to
Pueblo
and let the wind blow
right through me
in the parking lot
by the Trailways Depot

The Nike of Boone

for Randy Schroth

In America 1980
There are many Lost Zones   sad abandoned towns
Places left behind
By the movements of commerce

One of these is Boone
A hamlet where, out among
The long rattlesnake plains
Between the Federal Train Test Center
And 400 miles of straight nothing
One is suspended out of time

And there is nothing whatsoever left to do
Except stand around that little park in
The center of town
Actually just a large patch of burnt-out grass
Where the place of honor
Usually occupied in American towns
By a statue commemorating the local war dead
Is instead taken up by a vintage Nike missile
Gay souvenir of the Days of Ike
When things were still alive in Boone

The wind blows very hard around the tall white missile
Funneling up and down the open streets of tarpaper
Shacks and broken-down mobile homes. It leans a little. It may
Blow over if the wind comes on too hard
But that's no tragedy
Nothing's no tragedy in Boone—
In fact, nothing's no nothing.

What the Pioneers Always Wanted to Do Was Arrive

Which meant getting across the mountains alive
but then what? You lost track of the lessons
of the journey when the beginning fell out of sight
beyond the black unreeling truck lane of eternity

Out the window it helps to sing, Goodbye
to the pronghorn, and the buffalo
drops his shaggy head into the unreclaimed sage
unremarking our mechanized passage

Who at the end, may come to tread
the thick lawns of the Biltmore
which unravel from bungalow
to bungalow, trued perfectly
as strips of crushed money
leading to infinity

Standing on them, it will be possible
to look back to the east
and truly see nothing
of what we have crossed over
for the first time

Heartbreak Hotel

Stories Told by the Shores of the Lakes of Africa

While the cash-green palm fronds sway, tears round as coconuts tumble out of their eyes and roll down their gleaming breasts, finally toppling over when they reach the nipples, like big drops hitting the headlights of a Porsche streaming down the Pacific Coast Highway in the rain.

Character Is Fate

God was a woman. Mary was, frankly, God, John said. Yes, she was God; that was all there was to it. Falling in love with her had been like a religious conversion, John said. But you should not make a god out of another person. John was later to find this out the hard way.

Life Among the Canyons

Life among the canyons of Los Angeles. Explorers in jodhpurs and jungle hats drink gin slings on the porches of huts built on stilts. Cars pour up the freeway in the rain like homing salmon, ahead of the full lash of storm tilting in from the Pacific. Arriving home, we hear the women laugh. They run to fasten down the mats and hatches of batting and bamboo, their skin-covered breasts flashing as the water streams down them. We will give them diamonds and record contracts and they will sit for paintings. Our portraits of them will end up in a museum whose architectural character is geometrical and unfriendly. The curator will be twenty-nine years old and from the East.

Death, Revenge and The Profit Motive

Death is good, revenge is a waste of time, and whoever thought up the profit motive didn't understand either of those things, John said, tipping his head back to pour another drink into it. He was paying twelve hundred dollars a month to keep Mary in a glass and redwood shack with a hot tub in the hippest canyon in town, he said. And now she wouldn't even talk to him, and—he said—he was dying. "But only to get even!"

Heartbreak Hotel

Heartbreak Hotel is located among the abandoned oil derricks of Venice, California, on Feb. 15, 1954. It is a small bungalow with a white picket fence. A man in a dirty undershirt stands in an open window staring at us. Suddenly a chill wind blows across the oily surface of the grey canal. We look up into the sky, which has no color at all. It frightens us and we turn to leave but as we begin to run, our first footsteps are drowned in the loud strains of "Heartbreak Hotel," which the man in the window is singing in the window of the Heartbreak Hotel.

The Nelsons in San Roque

Those bungalows of San Roque
so perfect yet oddly sad
("a little wood & stucco
to keep the sun out")
always remind me of
where the Nelson family lived
way back in the days of Hi Oz
Hi Pop Hi Rick Hi David.

Everybody in that family was Okay
every day for a whole decade.
And when Ricky turned out to be
a low rider, it was still okay.
And that's the way it is today
among the petticoat palms
of Calle Noguera
and Puesta del Sol.

You can't rain on the parade
of the petit bourgeois
because it doesn't have one
except at Fiesta
when rain's against the law.

Things to Do in California (1980)

Play beach volleyball
Make surfboards & live at Dana Pt.
Pick up chicks galore
Shine it on & get a good suntan
Catch cancer from the chemicals in the water
Die a grotesque death
Have a movie made about your life
Make sure you look good in every scene

The Class Doesn't Struggle Anymore

Why is it so unsurprising that
the little man in the white coat
who drives the small motorized cart
across the manicured putting green
that grows like crushed money
between the bungalows of the Biltmore
doesn't appear to enjoy the acquaintance
of the thin old man in the Italian sweater
who emerges from one of the bungalows
tugged along by a tiny expensive dog?

Another Exotic Introduction

Nothing but psychodrama
and disillusionment
in the canyons of the wealthy

Still there's a swell sunrise
up Gibraltar Road a ways
where the red-yellow spectra
of the rising sun to the left (east)
swim up above the marine layer
starting down around Ventura County
and all Montecito's
hazed terrarial shadows erupt at once

The resultant sky is a story
of wild peach liqueur
spilled on dirty pillows

The Pack Approaches the Mission

The sun dies into pink smog off Goleta
and over toward Point Conception
the violet reptiles of the night
begin to slide across the sky
like pieces of neon tubing.
In such lighting the wild dogs
are held momentarily at bay.

The building blocks of a superior logic
seem to slip into place
with a quiet authority. The moon comes up.
There is a small click. It is evening.

It is of course the protected
evening of the very rich
who do not like to lean
into the wind. They stand, the pair
beyond the camphor tree on Laguna Street
bathing in its fragrance. Two old dames.
Perhaps they are not very rich after all.
It may be just the blue hair that fooled me.

It may have been the failing light.
It may have been the falling rose-colored
flowers of the pink flame tree,
or pieces of their pods,

which are covered with rusty wool,
that fell through the air
and affected my vision.

It may have been the pollen in the air,
the fluffy cotton heads which have
just burst from the floss-silk trees,
or floating strands of the dark
hair-like fibers that are
shed by the fortune palms
whenever the breeze arises.

There is a serenity about this apparition
but it is abruptly broken
by the peremptory bark of the pack-leader,
who, poised at the brink of the trees, signals
with a crazed snarl for the rest of the pack to advance.

Under the Fortune Palms

Some people think meanings are hard to find
In the 1980's decade of great emptiness
Among the bungalows of Samarkand
I stood under the fortune palms
And watched for a sign to blow by
In the throbbing Santa Ana
But all that came my way
Was the remote echo of a woman's voice
From down around Xanadu Street
Calling for her dog to stay

Off Goleta

Suddenly on the Mission lawn
A guy tosses a frisbee catching sun glints
Into the vermilion jaws of dusk
While above the frayed palms
A great sherry party takes place in the western sky
With catering by Giambattista Tiepolo
Eternity is in that moment
As if the sun were going down over Venice
And there one stood, *maestro di pintore,*
Calculating the finishing touches
Instead of only off Goleta

Dear Customer

Quit your gripes about the bad air
being the dead end
of civilization as known

According to *Rédiffusion du Sud*
it's only a serious case
of dissolution by aerosols
in *Le Cimetière Tropique*
where invisible particles corrode
the anti-frontiers
and leak a desert music
into the marine band

An advancing state
(in other words)
of post-Club Med tristesse
expressed thru the business end
of a Porsche exhaust pipe

More Crooked Lines from Paradise

for Dennis Cooper

If you've got a problem, come on over
It's like heaven up here
but you can get lost in the likeness
fumbling in a wet similitude through
too many consecutive turquoise days
tiptoeing around the corrals of the rich
leading up to the brink of the autopsy
sometimes it almost makes you wish
you hadn't died, so you couldn't dig all this

A Polyester Notion

We have reached the other side of the harbor
the sails of the yachts are slapped against the sky
like acrylic colors straight out of the tube
equally thoughtless and simple is the deep
lavender backdrop against which the ochre
mountains are flatly and theatrically stacked

We can keep on continuing along this line
as far as the grave of Ronald Colman or we
can double back and visit Ross Macdonald's
locker at the swim club though I seriously doubt
Robert Mitchum will be there what with
the polo season opening this week and all that

Lines Composed at Hope Ranch

"Twist away the gates of steel"
—DEVO

O wide blossom-splashed private drives
Along which sullen-mouthed little guys
In motorized surreys
Ride shotgun over spectacular philodendra!
O paradise of zombies!
O terminal antipathy to twist
And shout!
O hotel-sized garages
Inside which smoothly-tooled imported motors
Purr like big pussies under long polished hoods!
O fair haven of killjoys
United to keep surfers off
One of the great beach breaks
Of the West Coast!
O floral porticos, flowers
Of de Kooning, de Chirico
Chateaux! Estates where jokes
Aren't funny! What secret meaning awaits
Behind your stone and steel gates
Your walls of bougainvillea
Your date palm-lined roads
Your quiet oak-shaded lake
Like a European protectorate in Tanganyika?
Surely nothing disorderly, nothing disarrayed
Nothing at all except the great Pacific swell

Of money!

The Muses' Exodus

Out of the fading morning fog, in a powdery blue day
under the bays of the oak and the laurel
one can almost imagine the soft forms moving

to a hype that insinuates like music from a zither
deep there, out of the rocks, by the spring
where the oracle waits with lips pressed
almost as tight as the drawer of the cashbox

"Those men whom the gods wish . . ."

Those men whom the gods wish
to destroy, they first make
mad, and then, when the first white flecks
of foam speckle the men's lips—the spit
of bewilderment, of overpowering visions—the gods
throw their heads back and they
laugh and laugh, they laugh and they
laugh, until they are rolling on the floor
of the heavenly TV lounge

Sadly Céline

Sadly Céline
in death was spoken
of not so much
for the work which
brought with it
such inconsistencies
of character, as
for the latter. A

text is variously
a life, but the purpose
of an individual
is single.
To be difficult
is to be difficult.
There are no two
ways about it.

Wrong from the Start

The path of least resistance
is a straight line
but once you deviate
even slightly
the path of least
resistance becomes
that of greater
and greater
deviation

Identification Tags

Ghosts do wear sheets but not for sleeping.

Sometimes people die while still alive
and then come back to life
but only partially. You can read the signs
around the eyes, which get
a dusty look like burned out hundred watt bulbs.

When they pass one another on the streets
there is a soft noise, as of muslin touching.

Teflon and Velcro

To get ahead
in this world of ours
you've got to have
a hide as tough
and a head as hard
as Teflon
and in addition
you've got to know
how to hook into
the powers that be
as perfectly
as though they and you
were matching slabs
of Velcro

Say What?

As a principle of government
in an entropic democracy
plausible deniability
is undeniably plausible

therefore absolutely correct
and almost as good as
the ability to say what
you remembered to forget

Democracy

In the motel
room mirror

a yellow
light pulses

on polyester lips
pressed to sandwiches of hair

January 25

Lying here while she's not
picking out
stark empty-armed plum tree traceries
Sunday morning world still dark
after forty days of the world night
January 25
a vacancy in the matrix of creation

Into which bed returns the one unageing
eternal thing she's rounded sweet beauty that yet
undoes and wakes and separates
her own being from the world's
large and with its color
warm and moist and coming
green entry
as out the window in the scrub backyard
the small
dark red plum buds still furled in
to themselves on long thin finger
branches start to swell out

The Blue Dress

I close my eyes
and see you at the age of 30
beyond the mist of affect
in your blue dress
so slim and Viennese
in the Sharons' picture gallery
at Tissa's party
a stormy night in 1974
with the ocean roaring
against the breakwater
I find you there with
all my projections
withdrawn at last
and what appears is
you in your blue dress
in this bewildering recurrent
intensified mind garden
I call creation
because you created it for me

1987–1995

Arctic Cold Snap

The cherry ball on the mercury stick drops off at three zero
Off to the left the iridescent glow of the sea glances
Gold and hard in the thin indifferent sun
Ah and all the green and growing things wonder what hit them

Nasturtium hibiscus and clover shriveling
Noiseless as fear in a wide wilderness
This laser blast from the polar freezer fuses
Leaf arteries into obelisks of bright glass

Quivering in the coldwave's intenser day the Mind
Republic meanwhile narrows and darkens
Host to dim shades as the moon compels them on
Driven space ghosts before an enchanter fleeing

The long weight of light's pain-scored infinity
Keeps sleep from ever easing our agitated songs
Still tall redwoods charmed by the high volt stars
Dream and so dream on all night without stirring

As in the selfsame beat of time's broad wing
A lone jet roars by among the bleak grown pines
A light blot of grey water color bleeding
Spreading the deep possessed winter dusk across the land

The Possessed Winter Dusk

Possessed by phantom touch
I am tuned to your power station
Soprano sax sounds float in the cold blue dusk
Over East Bay hills' heavy green shoulders

Drawn by dark earth rising plants
Like some buffalo soldier on an Indian pony
I hold on to the night's dark mane
In the hollow bowl of the drum of your body

Solstice

Cold floating days, difficult to keep body
Temp. up as planet cools off mysteriously
This P.M. two small grey birds bump
Around in the rose bush for a while
A capella (no rush hour for once)
In last rays of tinny Christmas sun
While voluntary trumpets are quietly
Emitted by radio into Jerusalem foiled sky
Far off and to our great astonishment
O blue earth sounds your golden flower
From the bell of its silver horn
I didn't think it would ever come back on

Fractured Karma

Early morning light archery off a far boom shore
Thrust bellies to air fool moon's plum shades awaken
Beneath them voice and ghost curve away to ocean deeps
In the hollow bowl of the drum of the body

Moon pictures propped on the morning gestalt
A plum gray flood of light de Kooning would have killed for
Its full Rig Veda morning alarm glow rising
Like water bubbles into a drowner's mouth

Eternity Time Share Rebus

He is reclining like a river god on a rock
She is plucking a sweet olive branch from the moon palace
There is none of that sharp outline we think of as reality
A breeze drives wisps of fog across the pale moon
Like a thin wash of gray water color bleeding
Down into flat-topped fortune-telling plane trees
The joyous body chemistry bubble of youth
Breaks and we free-fall through the leaves
And when we land he is still reclining like a river god
And she is still waiting on the moon palace stairs

Seduction in the Wider Fields of Eternity

Psyche's clear lake riverhood shining looking glass cold
Mirrored my life back up to me from the depths of that hollow bowl

Where the gulf sky is separated from the gulf by a thin blue line
In the hollow bowl her body makes intersected by mine

By biological predetermination the ancient Egyptian
Word for kiss was derived from the verb to eat

A memory that vibrates long after the string is plucked
Creating a note sustained by the reverberating of her body

To fill to capacity the consciousness of the chosen one
So there is no escaping the ever rekindled hunger

Perishable Memo

I saw your body swim up the vivid night sky
A silvery white weight wet haired
Salmon breasting fire tides in silk swift ascension
While on the wide flowing black periphery
Wild stars flared out and showered
Failing to follow you in your higher leaping motion

But with my memory that fluid shape too will die
No one will see what I've seen
No one will go where I've been
Wan worlds from which the colors drained away
Leaving only these strange unearthly word outlines

Aqualung

Slow cling of gray white rain at oyster dawn
As if thin cloth were being continually torn
Inside outside, soft sizzle of wet rubber
Hugging four lanes of blacktop traffic back
Firing bridgeward over this slicing sluiceway
That cuts slick and gleaming as a blade
Through dull wool light leaking from blue pleura

Subject

distrusts all pasts
conditionals and perfects
future continuous too

suffers
fallibility of memory, senses
history is compound
of minute particles, questions
whether event exists
if unrecorded, hears noise

of one small plane
passing over rather high up
gradually diminishing into nothing,
                              cool,

lightweight

Tree Talk

Tree talk is the party line of the intelligent listening forest
Whether the smooth voiceless no breeze whisper rustling
Inside green upper tiers of a fogbound blue spruce
Or the deep aether growth song stirring
Down in each tender quiet working sub-earth redwood shoot

Inside the Redwood

Floating tiers and worlds
a green heaven doll house

dense microwood spaces
needle masses stretch out

big rain shroud wings over
air runways imagined solid

as clouds flown through in planes
thick stacked tufted landings

branch bales piled up feathery
no sky shows through

in there the greens so dark
like blacks with orange edged

light lower lift-ups
of needle tip droopers poised

to move up and down in
the water weighted wind

Linnaeus' Flower Clock

6 A.M.	Spotted Cat's-ear opens
7 A.M.	African Marigold opens
8 A.M.	Mouse-ear Hawkweed opens
9 A.M.	Prickly Sow-thistle closes
10 A.M.	Nippleworth closes
11 A.M.	Star of Bethlehem opens
12 NOON	Passion-flower opens
1 P.M.	Childing Pink closes
2 P.M.	Scarlet Pimpernell closes
3 P.M.	Hawkbit closes
4 P.M.	Small Bindweed closes
5 P.M.	Water-lily closes
6 P.M.	Evening Primrose opens

Linnaeus leaned forward on his hands
in a rhapsody of taxonomy
outside the medical faculty hall at Uppsala University
and knew the hour exactly
simply by glancing down at
the frail Moschatel or Town-hall clock
which bears at its stem tip five small flowers
four encompassing its perimeter
like the four faces of a clock
the fifth pointing straight up at
the sky habitation
of a tidy clockmaker god
on whose star circuits this whole vivid time garden was modeled

For Robert Duncan

d. February 3, 1988

How the arm moved
throwing the poet's
ashes out of the boat
how it all comes back

How the whole story
form of telling curves
the story around
these cosmic corners

How the stars swam
how the moon
was dying down
out over the water

To loosen out into
those big quiet waters
little pieces of
us all are floating on

As the Human Village Prepares for Its Fate

While everything external
dies away in the far off
echo of the soul
        still there's a mill wheel turning
it is like a good
kind of tiredness in
the moment before sleep
        by some distant stream
a note of peace
in a life which
will never be peaceful
        as the daylight fades
the dream disintegrates
but the shadow holds
no power
        over what's about to happen

The Lyric

Suffering
lament, sorrow and wild
joy commingle in

the lyric—a collective
sigh of relief comes cascading
out of the blue—

a yearning to submerge
in life like the swimmer
in the pool forgetful

immersed and quenched—
water trailing scattered
diamonds in a rustling

voice of resigned subsidence
as though in the same stroke
everyone alive were speaking through you—

Statue

The angel asked, as his shoulders were pressed into the stone
Why me? And taken from the inhabited body,
Like the lyric voice rustling from memory forests,
Childhood rushes toward death, a wind in those woods,
Crashing through trees, dying out,
Settling like a white mist over everything.

Nodding

Drowsiness, identity drifting,
some kind of white

flower seen through isinglass,
stupor, bliss,

the moment before sleep
as the foretaste of the moment

before death—experience
of space receding, forgetfulness,

fate a self held mesh
in time like dust in a net

through which breath sifts with
the same kind of wet thin

cloth to skin feeling
as of gauze or muslin

Energy of the Pre-World
as a Bungee Cable Jumper

Before the light radiates, where do you place it,
back there or out here in the pre-world
of street riot and armed detachments
grown commonplace, where the beam rotates like a mars light,
thought is as cautiously leashed as a bungee cable jumper

entrusted to a body beyond your body—is there
a body there, is it real, can you touch it
through the dark fire of the pre-world
that closes in? The presence of energy within
the elastic net fate weaves is the reckless

daredevil of the pre-world; fate allows it three
leaps, two snaps back, causing suffering,
causing hells; creating the body of desire,
suspending it in the vastness of space,
expanding it, disrupting it, offering it intense

resistance, whereof it can know itself.

Antiquarian

It is only mourning for the lost
Moment that has preserved like an echo of time
In these rustlings from the past
What the living moment continues to miss

A hieroglyphic scrap of extinct emotion
Set adrift down pathways of forgotten life
As the human village prepares for its fate
The dream disintegrates but the shadow holds no power

Moira

You must not change your life plan over
Divine airspace reserved for
Vector traffic of the ion
Charged hyper soul swarm

Through that void outer zone (cloud nebulae)
Where the radio frequencies (her messages)
Get lost in silence and a soft
Blue dust left by the memory of light

Day Detail—Low Light of Afternoon

Pleasant northeast wind, two monarch
butterflies being idly blown
through the ivy—airplane sounds,
traffic sounds, sounds of someone
hammering. Being, idly blown
from star to star on a spore
makes it across all that nothing
just to have a home, like the boll
weevil in the Leadbelly song,
just to keep from lying down alone.

"First cold winter twilights . . ."

First cold winter twilights despite this
week's Richmond refinery fire
never more perfect even the
burned and corrupt air stunning
saffron violet orange indigo
becoming blood red as sun descends
with a delayed shudder or retarded
tremor into ocean fire
and night begins to close in
over the whole sky from other
(eastern) end—a deep blue bowl

or dish inverted convex
glass dome extruded
pyrex lid over boundless
now starless ozone
depleted spaces of end
times—last hundred years of
human habitation?—rendering
in view of coming loss
earth in ever more damaged form
ever more beautiful than before

Final Farewell

Great moment in *Blade Runner* where Roy
Batty is expiring, and talks about how everything
he's seen will die with him—
ships on fire off the shoulder of Orion
sea-beams glittering before the Tannhauser gates.

Memory is like molten gold
     burning its way through the skin
It stops there.
                     There is no transfer
Nothing I have seen
will be remembered
beyond me
That merciful cleaning
of the windows of creation
will be an excellent thing
my interests notwithstanding.

But then again I've never been
     near Orion, or the Tannhauser
gates,

I've only been here.

Possession

"I have two luxuries to brood over in my walks,
your Loveliness and the hour of my death."
—KEATS TO FANNY BRAWNE, JULY 25, 1819

She was bedridden, befogged by brandy and
Opium, in pain, disheveled, beautiful,
And for the first time unarguably physically *there*
As he sat up long nights in the armchair,
A strange adolescent beside her strange body,
The only one of which he ever wished to take possession,
So that later when he huddled speechless in his grief
Behind the master's desk, and the whole class
Fell into a hush out of sympathy with his loss,
He knew they had no idea how unfortunate a one
He was, or what he would give to have her back—
His life, and the sexual form in which it possessed him.

Premonitory
(Keats, Teignmouth, Spring 1818)

Mariners don't think about the deeps too much.
The canvas of my reverie: maritime,
With promontory, cave, and little antique
Town that's emptied for a sacrifice.
A boat tacks round the cove and disappears
Into my mind's eye, where the scene plays over

And over: a small town beside an immense sea,
A white sail tacks around the promontory.
Mariners don't think too much about the deeps,
Poets were once thought premonitory.
The canvas of my reverie is
Maritime, with a promontory, a town:

The town has emptied for a sacrifice.
I close my eyes, but the same scene plays over:
Above the victim's head the priest suspends
A blade, light plays cleanly upon bronze,
The sun beats down, the confused heifer lows,
The pipe shrills, the bright libation flows,

Those of the faithful with weak nerves look away,
The blue paint splashed beneath a glowing sky
Bleeds across the harbor to the bobbing skiff
Whose white sail shows above the green head cliff,
Moves round the point, and seems to freeze in time
The unison hymn of sailors who forget

All that they know but their songs' chiming,
Chanting as we did when poetry was young,
Trying not to think too much about the deeps,
Our fear of death, and this abandoned town
Which itself has lost all memory of
The qualities of life vacated when we die.

Phosphorescence
(Keats, Hampstead, May 1819)

Beneath that darkling covert where the still
Invisible bird has built its nest in
Brown's garden like the bearer of a singing
Telegram arriving this forward spring

From a future I am not fated to be in
Life shows the magic hand of chance
At work in every little thing—not least
This tranquil song, whose joy fulfills my search

For the elegiac silver lining
Landing in my lap like this—just when my
Mind was most open to the glow that comes
Up like stardust from the things growing there

Weight
(Keats, Winchester, September 1819)

After another fine sharp temperate night
It is a warm morning. This is part of the world.
Summer light and dust blow yellow
Filmed clouds into the air. The brown stubble

Fields feel warm, give off a red excited
Glow like irritated raspberry marks
On fair skin, with its soft white weight,
As the doleful choir of gnats still wails,

And the maiden at the manor window shakes
The sheets out, or is it her fine light hair
That flows or is flung from the storybook casement,
That causes me to stop to catch my breath?

Melancholy Watch, the Downs
(Keats, September 1820)

My melancholy watch, mid-quarter-deck,
Drifting: I follow the play of gulls.
The sun is long gone down, the east darkling,
The ship drifts. In the west, some brightness remains.
Momently there are two flights of gulls moving
One to the east into the dark and one
Out of the west, in the last rays of the sun,
Left and right so entirely dissimilar
That the name gull quite falls from them
As I watch, and the chiaroscuro
Of the evening is torn open, altering
Everything: so that now everything is
Only itself: the gulls, myself closer
In nature than if I still knew their name,
Yet at the same time moving farther out,
Sinking deeper into a fading sky
Which soaks them up like ink accepting water,
Coaxing darkness out of reluctant night,
Bringing on the abolition of that false
Identity which made naming possible.

Keats: Coda: Echo and Variation

"The calculable law of tragedy"
—HÖLDERLIN

I

Mariners don't think too much about the deeps
Of the Other at the bottom of the ocean.
Like a sort of north star which in shining
Accelerates all my thought from far off,

Identity presses on me so all day
As to tease sleep out of my anxious mind.
Melancholy lunes, identifying with
Tom dismal and forlorn and spitting blood.

Heart, ever out of its element, keeps
Identifying with Hamlet, a dying
Sun beats down, the confused heifer lows,
Feeling nature's mass fall and spill like

A blade. Light plays cleanly upon bronze.
Above the victim's head the priest suspends
Our fear of death. And this abandoned town—
Where love melds into death, and vanishing

Sleep fills itself with ominous programs,
The whole fate drama hoving into view
Before dawn under the lyric stars—
Tacks around the cove and disappears.

II

A boat tacks around the cove and disappears
From the world on paper liberty wings.
At five o'clock of a summer morning
Sleep fills itself with ominous programs,

The whole fate drama hoving into view
Before dawn under the lyric stars.
She comes, she comes again, sighing like
Poetry and not any woman

I've floated with, through that melancholy
Marshlife of some primordial littoral
Where love melds into death, and vanishing
Riverine currents of language swirl

Like death on my tongue poisonous as
The word she breathes into me like a fate.

III

As time washes round these human shores
It must be poisonous to life itself,
The stubborn desire to find something outside
The perfidy of that deceptive voice.

Identity presses on me so all day
I'm obliged to go out, and when I come in
To somewhere even more crazy and strange
I plunge into abstract images to ease

Being in that circle of sad hell
Nature normally holds off from us.
A strange adolescent beside her strange body,
I can never forgive my mother for dying.

But everything's explained in advance,
What's planned falls away before what happens.

IV

The same old narrative of loss replayed
On her glowing sweat beaded shoulders,
The night wanderer pulled by gravity
Sinking into a desired release again.

Outside the gaslights of Gloucester Square went dark,
Street vendors came out to air their morning cries.
I and a pale lady seemed to swirl
Through hell space, joined at the mouth

While the slow making of souls overshadows
Every thing in this vale of sorrows—
Lovers floating and fading, all mindless,
Assassins of innocent nature—

My blood over-heats, the world-wind blows,
I must write to chase them from my mind.

v

She moves in next door, we huddle over
Paolo and Francesca in Dante: Fate
Floats through the whirling atmosphere
Of the sexual, and is consumed

While in Hampstead the god keeps being born;
Sweet surrender tastes like poison in my mouth,
My blood over-heats, the world-wind blows
Every thing in this vale of sorrows

Through the whirling atmosphere of hell
To London, depression, withdrawal—
Warning, betrayal and death deep
At work in every little thing—seeing

London as Atlantis, that sunken city
Sifting like glittering dust through the stars.

VI

The moving waters at their priestlike task,
Polaris growing brighter against the sky
Like an evening glory, with Vega
Swimming, an incandescent sea of gas

That surrounds its central star the way
A modal continuum of quiet
Keeps the Ring Nebula in Lyra spinning,
Show the magic hand of chance at work:

She moves in next door, we huddle over
The doomed infatuated ones in Dante,
The burden of the mystery producing
A mimetic touching of the strings

With which we might identify
Deneb and Altair locked across the dark.

VII

The night wanderer's pulled by gravity
Through hell with a beautiful figure whose lips,

228

Those flowers of death's close growth and breathing,
Glow like irritated raspberry marks
Once the swarming of phenomena begins.

The story of Paolo and Francesca
So spooks me my heart's too small to hold
The elegiac silver lining
Once the swarming of phenomena begins
To wed your loveliness with the hour of my death.

We dine, and our fate is sealed. Like a recurrence
The doomed infatuated ones in Dante
Who cannot see what flowers are at their feet
Once the swarming of phenomena begins
Cry out into the archaic Saxon dusk

Where ecstasy once poured forth, with
Shadowy thought left to supply its own
Sheath of feeling in which I hang all through
That aching starlit spring in Hampstead,
Once the swarming of phenomena begins.

VIII

When I say "I" it isn't *I* I mean,
This idle, empty scarecrow figure,
Unborn thing in its larval sac suspended,
Though I am forever stretching out my hand

229

When I know all thoughts ought to be on you—
Better perhaps to guess than to see
Poetry in the mimetic touching of
A future I am not fated to be in—

The brevity of life, its tenuousness—
Faint luminous phosphorescence, rising
Desire—myself the hunted one consoled—
To slip the grasp of a familiar ghost

Causes me to stop and catch my breath,
Happy when I am alone and not myself.

Like Real People

The cry of a lost soul clowning yet meaning it
Shatters the silence of the planetarium
But the sky isn't falling. No wolf's at the door.
Still there's that echoing voice. Watchman, what of the night?
It's spherical, inky and as big as Kansas.
The moon is not quite round. Several stars come out
Of the backdrop and simulate topology,
Boring as old photos are yet absorbing as
They also are—potentially embarrassing
Like real people, who, when they confront themselves
With the dolorous anthems of that humdrum
Self awareness tolling in the middle distance,
Dismiss its alarums as mere background noise,
The cry of a lost soul clowning yet meaning it.

Getaway Package

The long vacation turns into a way of life
The nervous beauties of the seasons amble
Precisely past like flamingos or mannequins
Commissioned by the gods to keep the view
Ever various in its several lights
To edify just this one tender watcher
Who smiles at them as she adjusts the picture
Observe how seemingly radical the way
They've modified their old rude manners
The way in which when she inspires their mirth
It almost looks as if they're falling over
Each other in an absurd effort to please her
As though whether or not it's in her interest
They'd do anything to keep her here

Happy Talk

To repeat herself's nature's way to teach—
Need's ancient sentence of soft apposition
The rumbling of some deeper understanding
Juliet's comment on tortoiseshells ("They're all dumb")
Notwithstanding, being an affection sponge
Is not an unintelligent quality.
The ability to accept physical
Expression, straight across, no questions asked, is
Not this genius of a kind? Deep breathing,
Forepaws kneading, eyes squeezed shut in pleasure squint,
Dark Sister forms herself into a comma,
Thick brown belly fur cradling my plying hand
To bring forth this low down voicebox motor hum
That keeps on coming—happy talk, nature's speech—

Christmas on Telegraph

Shoppers rush past frozen images unseen,
In bright synthetics Sierra skiers ski
Through snowdead woods on blurred storewindow TV.
In the forest it is cold. How can it be
Colder in the cities? Street people crouched
Under Amoeba's protective arcade mouth
Such big round starving O's: oxygen balloons
Lifting off to perfect freedom, no strings—
A pity they can't float off in them.
Peace, brother. I can spare the buck or pass it.
Just breathing commits one to everything—
To life—which can't be purchased on this street
Where ravenous as sheer presence Christmas lights
Up human appetites for guilty pleasures.

Through This Long Winter
of Freakshows and Floods

Our school a play, the play a carnival
In which the fool was me, the clown was me,
Mentor and tormentor in one role
Leaving you to wow the class, girl sawn in two,
Leaving me, that comic character, stranded
As the waters rose, me and that scrawny cat,
Half wild, on our raggedy raft in the flood,
An upside-down bumbershoot afloat above
Air ducts, vents, chimneys, TV antennae—
And when the raindrops weirded down
From unindulgent heavens threatened
Finally to engulf us, that little cat
Jumped in a pan set out to catch leaks
And started rowing toward morning

To the Mistress of the Sailor's Rest

The antiquarian spirit sown in you
By your years among these splendid wrecks—
The venerable Capt. Gimp, his grizzled,
Toothless, brandy-breathing mate; the ship's
Surgeon, an addict with an erring knife;
The idiotic cabin boy, poking with
Idle digit every crevice below decks;
The blunt armorer, blazing at forges
Long consigned by history to scrap;
The daft sailmaker, whose billowy canvas
Illusions are to these leaden wharfside skies
What poems once were to real life,
And are about as much use to it now—
Will pave your days with doubtful sunken treasures.

Old Album

No past bears presents to equal being here.
Put that book away. Ghost faces, doubtful gifts:
Word apparitions washed ashore to perish
As life roars by in blue reverie blurs,
Tulips incandescent as the rain that beats them
When March storms unleash this wild dance of forms.
Presence comes before being, being before
There was ever a you or me. Ancient
Grief will go from you as from sorrowing songs
Sorrow goes, leaving nothing for you
To whom everything belongs because your poor
Defenseless inner self has gaily sailed
Into the room like all the modern languages
Coming down to us, so you could say these things.

On the Beach

The storm has ended and death steps back
Into the waters once more. All our troubles
Are behind us once and for all.
The moon looks down in single glory.
The apocalyptic view of the world
Supposes things do not repeat themselves.
But they do. And they do. And they do.
The sky clouds up. A new storm comes on.
Apocalyptic thinking presumes
All this has never happened before
And will never happen again. I know,
As the moon beams down on the photo-plankton,
All this will never happen again, too.
Wisdom is cold and to that extent stupid.

Torn from an Old Album

Pale intent wondering little
man with serious fedora
casts short shadow in flat wide
light of his grandfather's front yard
squinting dutifully into
a doubtful future's narrowing
eye. Years of rain and snow and sun
rush by, a blinding prospect. Night
falls and everybody dies
back into the faded album
pages, white blurs effacing youth's high

gloss. Loss, not yet more than a word
for what you simply can't find—toy,
book, sock—lurks unprepossessing
as among shades huddled ahead,
consciousness emerges: time stuns
it with one blow, stands it back up
so as to knock it down over
again. Still life continues to
play hopefully into the hand
behind the lens, fighting against
blinking; and then the shutter clicks.

1995–2005

from EMPIRE OF SKIN

(A poetic history of the Northwest Coast fur trade)

1. APPARITIONAL CANOE

a singing   wind rushed

                                through cedars

            silver moonlit

        beached whale   gleamed

out on the Sound

                    wave washed

otters slept on kelp beds

                back floating

2. MILD

They're easy together

                    inside the pod

when there's no hunting

the yelp of the little

one is not heard   on good days

when the weather is mild they move

        like the vowels in the word

                    repose

off shore to browse

        among sea

                urchin and mussel

            encrusted submerged reefs

or in drifting patches of

            floating kelp

3. BEFORE CONTACT

Indian wars and yet
peace in every upstream elbow of the inlet

In early summer the sea is glassy calm
fog banks form on the margin of
the Japan current, out offshore, where
sea otters swim,
and roll in day after day, morning
after morning,
breaking up only when a slight
breeze arises

the evil star dawning
with the white
sail on the horizon

4. LANDFALL

The first thing the sailing man
from the old world saw   after nearly going
fathoms down on unseen offshore
reefs underwater ocean ridges outlying
were rocks and shingle beaches
long Pacific rollers broke and roared
peaks clad with dark spruce and fir
and crowned with snow rose
to clouds which distilled sea borne
moisture down in showers day long
behind the outer margin
of beach the undergrowth spread
dank and impenetrable
as a native mind

5.   THE WATCHMAN

The Indian sentinel
at Point Lookout—
in pines, the wind rush—
saw white sails
—apparition
of a supernatural creature?
a great horizontal canoe
was rocked like a skiff

the wave wash
pushed its sound back
through the whisper
of wind in the trees

as the canoe was beached

("history" begins with this)

6. DRIFTING

Well we should have known
it was all over with cant of empire
those snowy diamond mornings up
at the top of the world
above the Sound's unnavigable reaches
that sky looked so clean and true
just because the air's so
clear at that altitude
Rousseau couldn't have foreseen
these unimaginable latitudes
from the ship the peaks
brooding above impassable inlets
we sent the pinnace up
that came drifting back down empty

7. AND THIS ALSO SHALL BE GIVEN US

Beneath the tawny port of a warm sundown
Clouds in the masts take on the structures
Exemplified in thought by a woman's bones
Calm lies the Sound under Venus rising
Orange goings down of great suns prelude
The light in which a flying fish catches them
Nights of the ocean in which your shrouding's
Caught as if it were in its own reflection
Your cruise having lasted all this long while
There are the summer night's Scarlatti
On the quarter deck under Pacific stars
And skins coming aboard in slim canoes
A coat of otter fit for a mandarin
In exchange for fishhooks and teapot lids

8. OLD CANTON

Fresh from the savage wilderness how strange
Old Canton! The terraced hongs
With their great go-downs out in front
Screening foreign-devil eyes from the Forbidden City,
Before which flows the Pearl River, bearing dreams!

Mandarin boats move up and down the river slowly
Barging into vision with gay pennants flying,
Propelled by double banks of oars
Moving up and down in hypnotic, stately cadence,
Like pagodas sailing into a busy paradise.

Great tea-deckers, topsides brightly lacquered yellow and red,
Squares of brown matting rigged out for sails,
Hauling Souchong, young Hyson and Bohea,
Pass down the aisle of darting sampans,
Each one housing an entire family of floating tradespeople.

Twilight falls, as clouds of red and orange spill across the sky,
Driving the boat people to their moorings,
A simple bamboo pole thrust in the oozy bottom.
Paper lanterns diffuse a soft glow over the river,
Blunt prows of opium skiffs begin to bump against the ship's sides.

9. SUPERIOR ORDERS (OCTOBER 1789)

"Haro: I have departed Nuca by superior order to San Blas"
  —Estéban José Martínez

The long love that in my thought doth harbor
How far from port with how much longer to go
For that matter how far from sherry or madeira
All that is lost and fallen ought to be
Who'd explain loyalty to fate and brandy
Indians among our crew dispirited by the cold
So much harsher than autumn in Mexico
Days of obscurity and foul prevailing weather
Rain fog and the progress of worm in planks
Closing off whatever had appeared our goal
We'll abandon everything we've built or meant to
Though the rice begins to produce the wheat is planted
All through the long New World shadowed afternoon
We warp out of the cove preparatory to sailing

Earthshine

The waxing crescent moon with furred nimbus
Of a cold milky mouse grave October
Blurring into blue dark Mare Nectaris
Endymion ringed with pearly fog
Mare Crisium and Mare Undarum
Old moon yearning in the new moon's arms
Every loose thread left dangling
At dusk Saturn rises out of the ocean
Heavenly waters so tired of waiting
Aquatic constellations swim into view
Aquarius Capricornus Pisces
Venus ascends four A.M. with the tide
White day opening not that far behind it
Swallows tossed wide around a calm sky

On the Playing Fields

Cold clear days with a kind of white haze
The eternity of thought against
The momentariness of sensation shows
Separation is all there is left to
Enact as the sky of evening closes
On each strained thud of a weary puppet heart
The calm that nature breathes grows large
Colors of an insect's wing on pale clouds
Serrated and recessive barred
A vapor trail cuts across a star's reflex
While eastward others now begin to sparkle
And as on the playing fields night conquers
The moon floats up cloaked in misty vagary
The blood aswarm with imagined lights

Prolepsis

Melodious liquid warble in the plum
Tree tells the sinking year how to feel
Its recession into grief as if a thorn
Poked a nester in an old wounded heart
Of stone from which slowly drips recognition
All breathing passion far above
These days atonal as white noise
Through bare branches cotton clouds drift by
Last yellowed leaves catch lone rays of sun
Going down into the motherless ocean
A light plane buzzes off toward brown hills
As shade drops over the next urban plot
To prepare the air for what the dead don't know
How swiftly we are coming to join them

Elegy

It's a pity we have to suffer
The bluejay said to me with a wink
If any part of the body be cut off
No part of the soul perishes but
Is sucked into that soul that remains
In that which remains of the body
These aren't tears anyway just eye gunk
And you've always taught me to be brave
As the last kindly rays of February
Sun warm bare ruined plum tree choirs
And light them up with a gaggle of buds
From which a few white blossoms are just
Starting to pop open as traffic hums
And in this moment there is nothing lost

Surrender

for my parents

"that strange indifference which we feel towards our relatives so long
as they are alive, which makes us put everyone else before them . . ."
—PROUST

The objects upon which their lives rubbed off
Some patina of a thousand tender hopes
From which the morning gladness had not yet gone
Some monument to pure hearts poor few keepsakes

Surrendered into the hands of bereaved
By departed hardly planned perhaps
Unconscious transmission aura of past
Which harbors within the shored fragments

Cargo cult histories hardly worth saving
Except they did as people do mid loss hold
Back something—self's drive to memorialize
Itself? not finally lose everything

Some last thing to be remembered by some sign
(*I was here*) at all cost not to surrender
That last claim on life don't forget us they cry
From that other world of grey light and shadow

Hold out spectral this sad sack of clues to
That communion of tensions their marriage was
His golf clubs his bond trader's card the sacred
Heart medal she kept the prayers to St. Jude

Helper of the hopeless her watch his AA card
One cufflink a kissoff note from a client
Two or three letters they exchanged her trip
To St. Paul her loneliness her "condition"

(Four months pregnant with me) respected
By everyone in the club car of the train
Ordered a scotch but sat there couldn't drink
Alone and thinking (cross with him?) all the way

Her letters of contrition his calls
Their reunion the child comes along
His drinking failure as a bond trader
High blood pressure Douglas Aviation

Humiliating years in sales his sample
Case of cardboard product containers
Her Andrea del Sarto Holy
Family bedroom wall decoupage

The image she died under in the room
In which they through my childhood fought and wept
Against "the condition" God each other
While I cowered in a crack across the hall

The photos of them honeymooning
In Wisconsin the only photos I've
Ever seen of the two of them together
Her hair twisted up at the top like Olive Oyl

His arm around her before the Queen's Bench
Her seven miscarriages later
Babies born dead jobs lost hopes shot blown
Lives woven together down life's crooked trail

His t-square his honorable mention
For cartooning his level a photo
Of him about eight in soldier hat
Holding a much too big for him bicycle

Hopeful on a street somewhere Chicago
Her father's gold badge his watch some beads of
A rosary her novena book holy cards
Marking her father's death her mother's his hers

So loss times loss still factors loss I don't
Know where I'd find his bones her "cremains"
Scattered by my brother over the snow
Over the frozen backyard grass my outfield

For marble ball little bat boyhood games
For love is human merely to surrender
The site yet clutch the objects of memory
Left me us here tearful holding the bag

Trinity

That early Trinity, my soul, my
Mother and my father whom I am
Advancing past his age to become
As I remember him, fleeing from myself,
Is still with me, hidden beneath hot eyelids.
In dreams she too speaks to me invisibly
But from above, getting fainter now as more
And more of her children die unborn, unloved
In the broken hands of awful father earth.
Batter my heart, three-person'd pronoun
For the first part of the life sentence pieces
Equally with the last part, never
Harkening to the parenthesis between.
Whatever agonies the body suffers pass.

Childhood

The time-crinkled photo of the snow
Suit boy in blizzard with big shovel
Who does not yet know he's to pose problem
For self family and wider world
Only that his purpose is to shovel snow
But having in a wink flake-blinded
Leapt into exactly that white world—
Was it what went wrong? Or that rightness—
Those white designs which childhood fosters
And the thoughts of each harmless hour
And only seeing through a long night
The snow falling all around the edges
Of the world—and low breathings coming after
With footsteps almost soundless in the blank drift

Little Bang

The night was hot and heavy and the single arc
Flared from the dark rising lamp city
Like a star that ignites itself on banks
Of some unlit river, spending on objects
More revelation than they are worth,
As time's vague vista opens up through
Successive rooms we've dumbly cruised among
In possession as we've never quite been
At the witching hour, though now there's little bang
Left to relish, nothing much, just these same vague
Vistas, all lost, receding the way the man
On the Jupiter mission got littler
And littler, and as we, older, grow closer
To other spheres than to that earth we recall

Light Sleeper

As all the ballast of familiar life
Floated away from the hot air balloon
That was taking me in far-travelling mood
Over vast still mountains once glimpsed in dreams
I felt my foolishness in the domain
Of the air like a kind of punctuation
Applied to a page before a word's written
By that great Friend who, scattered everywhere
In the universe, seems to piece together
The floorplans of the endarkened rooms
Of this great city by negative design
Until the shapes before my eyes became
Obscure as all those lost relationships,
As all the ballast of familiar life

Out of the Fog

sleep addressed me familiarly, calling

she takes a third of our lives and when

we come back this way a second time
        doesn't recognize us

traipses to the curtains to let
        in the broken glass light of clouds

        CLOSED

    read the sign on the dream shop door
    the battered mouse   a grey dust ball
            about two days dead

roared about lost innocence
        to a loose sock   on the closet floor

   ripped anew

        out of the upside
           down canoe

            (sleep's protection)

Children of the Future

The poor remedy of days can't ease us
Nor afford us line to fathom bottoms
Whose profane history's not yet clear—
That some authors speak of running years
Others of time down on its knees, panting, spent;
That there are as many great things perished
And forgotten as are now remaining here,
Vexed and perplexed in thought and precept,
Uncertain, doubtful and conjectural
As when evening shuts in to overtake
The world with darkness and, blinded,
After the long night of this world, we miss
The break of day into which light hurls
Wounded children, unable to hear or speak

Footsteps

Some crisis of a ruthless order
Must have driven us all off into our warrens
Of private dilemma and compensation
In subjective device, dressed up as
Lifestyle I don't doubt given the rue
With which if not to be even greater
Fools we must look back upon a protracted
Adolescence, squeezed into corner pockets
The knowledge of the subject becomes
Actual just at the moment there's this
Hollow sound of knocking at the door
Followed by footsteps of some singular
Person withdrawing on his or her own
Into whatever constitutes the future

Bach's Booty

Three barrels of beer was Bach's pay. Still now
A dim shadow falls across the bright festal tone
As we follow the figured bass part down
Memory lane, where the art form's short term losses,
Simulating his disputes with authority,
Preclude the purple laurels victory brings.
Don't blow your wig, scholar. Let the beer fiddlers play
"The Warrior Minstrel of the Forlorn Hope."
Life remains long, but now and then as the silver
Chords gather and are sprinkled above the planet
Like sparks pinned to a blue velvet canopy
We get these inklings, self regard drifts away
From boreal winter night's cold lucid frame
Into postromantic darkness, and real stars come out.

To the Muses of a Certain Age

Interesting autumnal inventory
Of winter faces, with leathery skin
Lank as an otherwise empty wallet
In which a check on fond nostalgia
Awaits the long belated cashiering
Of times out for old sergeants in a shade
Where mouths are holes worn into heads whence each
Tooth to a several destination's gone,
Let's let, since it's sink or swim anyway,
Our love descend onward over the falls
Not panting after life preserving beauties,
Able to ebb on later in the eddies
As a raft once pneumatic yet still clutched
Contributes even deflated to valor's
Anti-honeymoon a counselled rescue

Night Sky (March 23, 1997)

for Angelica

Sitting up on the roof with you on the night of the magic sky

The old reiterated queries, will you perish? will you fade?

Themselves for a moment fade and

Perish as the first contact occurs

For the moon passes through the penumbra but only partly through
　　the umbra before emerging

And during this time it appears bluish or greyish brown

Then later a dull coppery orange glowing inside its own aura, ancient
　　disc or coin

Rays of light just grazing the rim of our blue globe

Must be slowing down as they pass through these dense atmospheres,
　　whence they undergo

Refraction and, bent into the shadow cone,

Fall upon the eclipsed moon and give

It this eerie coppery glow against the deep

Blue black of the night—literally unearthly

Like Marvell's orange lamp in a green night

For these rays must also undergo

Through these rapt hours of our watching

Absorption in the atmosphere

The lower their path the greater absorption

Suffering greater and greater loss

In the blue and violet end of the spectrum

Exactly as though the sun were going down

On this now coppery or blood red moon
The full moon of the beginning of the thirtieth year of our union
In the midst of these years of greater and greater loss
Which appears to become perfectly
Round yet somehow swollen taut to bursting
Like the ancient blood oranges in the Sultan's garden
In the old walled city of Fez
Glowing darkly in the blue green depths of the leaves
And now it's sunset on the moon
Some places shading into yellow
Some into a dull red
Touching everything with a luminous aura or halo
And every feature stands out in relief
Like seeing you accidentally naked today
The blond lunar globe of your belly
Words can't convey the strangeness
A dull red disc apparently bathed in the glow
Of some celestial inferno
Set like a jewel in the sky full of stars
Which the full moon's normal brilliance would keep us from seeing
While just above it Mars appears unusually bright
And also orange in its glowing
Even as disappearing behind the large evergreen
To the pacific (ocean) edge of the roof rushes
The fuzzy starlike brushstroke in time of the comet Hale-Bopp

from COLD SPRING: A DIARY

22ND DAY

As we grow old
even the length of the day
may make us wet-eyed.
Deep grief
for the nature of things.
We walk single file
along the railroad track
in the wildflower field,
by the sandy beach,
in the short spring night.

23RD DAY

The slow spring day.
Slow days passing,
Accumulating.
Other days that are no more.
Tiresome thought.
A lot of gibberish.
This also is spring tranquility.

24TH DAY

Inmost mind,
new balance
soles shot,
socks show through
a springlike concentration.
Calm days,
the swift years
forgotten
for one minute
this spring morning!

25TH DAY

The world is still and quiet through fog.
A spring day begins.
In my hut, there is everything.
Outside, a three-foot garden.
A creek trickles past.
Ha—a spring lie!

26TH DAY

A long day.
My eyes are weary.
O, the days that are no more.
So glad they're over.
The cat drifts in sleep
beneath the sound
of the spring wind
in the redwoods.
The raccoons rumble on the roof.

27TH DAY

The morning expedition.
Baby sparrow
under the sink
leaks little chirps.
Mind in the way.
Mr. Worm is coming.

28TH DAY

I have heard the call
of the spring wind.
Sparrows are chirping
in the light evening rain.
Hearts full of fears,
they fly up and down.
Sneezing, why do
I lose sight of them?

29TH DAY

It's the long morning
of spring,
whittled down
by the spring rain.

30TH DAY

When I felt the spring rain
falling on my head
through the hole in the roof
I went out into the garden
knelt down
shed stupid tears
at the foot of the century tree
smelled things under the ground
turning to mulch
then went back inside
and listened to the distant sound
of ocean waves
pounding against the shore
in the spring rain.

For Ed Dorn

The passes over & through which I've
      been driven by you, Edward,
            are bright & shining, in

my mind. The prairie
      dog we visited, in my mind
           now that you've gone

(8:30 P.M. PST
      12/10/99) reminds a traveler
          is a man alone,

in a long coat,
      on a dusty prairie,
          walking on water

because the desert is now closed.

               1:28 A.M.
               12/11/99

Farewell Sweet Prince

The sun shone for you in the winter afternoon
Brightness fell from the air
Your pain was finally over
After thirty crazy hours of holding you
A fool who can't let anything go
I finally found the strength
To wrap your beautiful jungle body
Snowy belly afloat with lavender and cyclamen and roses
Furled in an old blue towel you liked to slumber on
And laid you in the ground
Beneath that old plum tree you used to bask lordly
Under and ponder the frantic squirrels

8:30 A.M.
12/27/99

The Spell

The day of the dead when
the veil between us and them
is thinnest   eyelash
kitty breath   umbrella flutter
psychic butterfly—

A whole procession of them coming
pushing through the net—the sugar candy
shedding of the skin and how
it lets the wind blow through the veins
the dance of the skulls and when
the spinning of the little mechanic
inside the toy clock stops
the dark man carrying two suitcases
steps from the now no longer moving train—

That's the day when
I know someone will be
no longer waiting,
the unborn child said.
I invented what I wanted to say
in case anybody out there,
on a cold grey day in autumn,
wanted to hear the thoughts
of the dead—
I opened the door and
in flew a moth, thinking
twilight came early

Another Obscure Reverie

Kitties came and went all night long
                2:30–5:30 A.M.
as in a curious furry nightmare
moth fluttering around the room in the dark
way too late
        for the radiant world . . .   or is it?

That's the sphere of the lux and
                the lumen, spurned
at your own risk—
the dark and the strange, or luminous
           and unlucky

Little Hymn to Athene

This morning   post storm

                                sky

the world got a good wash   now

                 the sea green

depths conceal a cold and clean

heaven   that by remaining

      YOUR ZONE

(thus hidden)   mimics

     your austerity flags

        coming out of the bath

shivering

before your epheboi

me a dim votary (burnt out bulb)

          standing under

the cold shower of your cosmic aspect

All Thought

What's all this commotion, as of
king-wings in migration
a strange fluttering in the boughs
in the great night of souls

In the little oak grove
out back the dying
plum is choked out
by the young oak

Above, the vast blue
climbed by a cloud-wall
suggests all thought's
supplanted

Drifting

A trumpet vine
a bright green
tree fern—the
violet light
of early evening
fog enshrouds
pink big
city clouds

Hope

Mare's tail clouds cotton white
against a summer yacht blue
sky—the extending of light into
the renewing of the evening

Vagabondage

Summer night
klang of stars

inner acoustic

water diamonds
                around
the oars

Message in the Fog

Aim high
like the sequoias—
aspire to
our most wild dipthong,

one solitary
roosting
sooty grouse
hoots

Vow

Goblins from the great star rebus haunt and run
Crushed leaf writing bleeds evergreen on the rock
Miles to reel backward before awaking
Thoughts, dreams, memories, reflections
The blue spurt of a lighted match
Flowers in the kerosene dark morning
Spooky cloud lights, layers of white shadow
The torn sail flapping inside the vast empty hangar
Blood, bone, marrow, passion, feeling
When the day grows calm I will begin my work

In Water World

The sea repeats itself in dreams, a green-grey world of water
Calm boats frozen in shade
Pale blank clouds, pines, rocks and kelp shrouds
Like woolly fish in mist pink distance floating
The beach stretches as far as the sand bar
Clean detached waves wash over dry stone, tears of rain drift
The water is perfectly still, restructuring everything

Intermittent Tempest

The rain should be able to understand your tears
The moon appears through clouds between fingers of cypress
In the whirlpool after the shipwreck

Dry leaves drift and blow over blue sand
A heavy curtain opens upon fogbound birds
Retarded clouds trail past unconcerned

And a low pressing voice in the wind
Disturbs the variable calm of the summer night
Drowning out the words to which the moon would have wished to listen

The Day Goes on Forever

We're alone my shadow and me
You're alone with your shadow too
The first day and the last day the same
First song same as last song

The stream weeps passing under concrete
Habitual deer have retreated
The earth is covered with vehicles
Meant to secure the unknown against us

The caged bird said this place is very pretty
Excellent for lunch fine for sleeping
But if I might ask one thing more
How come nobody thought to put in a door

All Souls

The moon coming through the curtains
makes geometrical patterns in bars
a calligraphic grid through which pass
the ever vigilant ones
the souls of "my" dead though of
                    course they're no one's
not even their own any more   merely
messengers of the mirror negative
dispatched from a mute past
to efface a haunted present
Would lighting up a stick of sandalwood
                        or cedar
give them speech? In the anxious distance
            of abstract nights and days
all souls float close enough to touch
in the half dark of the match scratch
and candle flicker
yet just (and forever to stay) out of reach

Another Sleepless Night

for Kenneth Koch

Who in this bowling alley bowled the sun?
Who made it when it rises always set
To go at once both down and up?
Who fashioned the curtain rods for this tapestry?
Who hung it there in the first place?
Was it the same hand that milked the great cow
Whose arched back forms the top of the sky
And whose hooves tapdance on the planets?
Who lit the twinkling lanterns that guide the cow home?
Who welcomes her with sweet grass when she arrives?
Who tends the fields where that grass grows?
Who stands amid those fields in a clearing
Where there is an ornamental fountain
And a sundial engraved with an ancient motto
And attempts to parse out all the angles
Of the growing shadows of the day?
Who mops his brow and wonders what
Day it is what week what month and what year?
Who held the mold in which this world of time
Was cast into this particular shape?
Who laid the corner stone? At whose command?
Who did these things? Who was he? Or she?
And why do I keep asking these questions?
Is it because I'm trapped in a universe warped

Out of its intended normality
By some remote unconcerned force? Does anyone
Else know? If so, who? And what can they do?

Why Hillary Became a Goddess on the Night of Her Acceptance Speech

Because her hair looked cool

Because some of the best alien minds are watching developments
    closely

Because she is the traditional Daisy poised fragile before the
    masculine mills

Of production, yet wearing out six black pants suits

To bring us to acculturation and consequence

Because the Nasdaq is plunging and there is a mandate for change

Sweeping through the gentle bacteria that make their home in her
    tireless campaign shoes

Because the worried market takes comfort in knowing what it
    must consume

Because choosing is not an issue except to the terrified cartoon
    eyeballs

In the take-out carton, wondering whose turn is first

Because some of the best alien minds consider "us" the
    shrill-voiced uncertainty factor

That threatens to bring the whole cosmic chorus to its whispering
    knees

Because Utopia is the island in time that forgot itself as it lifted its
    utensil

At the altar of its great consuming goddess No Memory, with her
    sadclown smile strained

Because her lofty position at the social fulcrum which is the mercy
     seat
Takes a terrific toll on black pants suit bottoms
Because some of the best alien minds are surveying developments in
     numb disbelief
Because 65% of the wood lice aren't losing any sleep at all
Because retreat in the face of even greater problems,
While not a bad idea, won't solve anything
Because acceptance and consumption are just what the market needs
To shake it out of its trance-like belief in what it thinks alien minds
     are saying
Because acceptance means acculturation to the masculine mills
Because happiness is merely their invention anyway, because Dame
     Pleasure is wearied
Of Earth, has taken to the air, faded, fluttered down in a still, snow-
Like inwardness to spill, scatter and be raked up with all the sibyl's
     other fallen leaves
In this enchanted-recount self-enclosure, like a small-town autumn
Where the commoners lie down nightly with what they have made
Happen, amid the bedded reeds of the vigilant event horizon
Because in this collapse its truths are received
By their souls, because of what this means to the odd weightlessness
     they feel
Because they have no way to grace their laurels
Beyond filling up the best alien minds, intent upon those peerless
     screens
With the black pants suits of our resident historian
Who's just keeping a chair among the blond clouds warm for them.

Venerable Imp Rebus

Frequently asked question: why won't he give up?
Old man Souxing, the longevity star god
An image of my craft, mapped between
Huckster and author, scholar and pickpocket,
Magician of symbols and plowman of Mt. Bank.
After three thousand years, the peaches have at last
Begun to ripen. The peach blossoms fall
Floating parachute-light on grey soft air
To the jade-green, then still black waters; slowly drift
Downstream. As if time were no element
In the world that is forming from this image
A small monkey sits on a large lotus, nibbling
A ripe peach. Souxing's on the shore: slouchy
Ancient bald gent with enormous cranium
Hinting of acromegaly, or vast thought?
The stringy hillbilly whiskers gape
Upon a bloated hairy winebelly,
The loopy walrus mustache droops into
A benign (or impish) trickster grin,
In his palm, a fat ripe softball-sized peach:
It's the peach of immortality. He guards
Over the well-being of this collapsing household
In which dwells the old poet-liar who finds in
The longevity rebus excuse to go
On waiting; does a peach branch sag toward his hand?

Bookmark

for Angelica

Old clichés finally speaking untold volumes,
"Getting on in years," that comedy without laughter,
Drifting through the fitful intervals in
Which insomnia presages a dull oblivion,
Half dozing, I am awakened suddenly
By the sharpness of the aromatic root
In your name, which has your fragrance in it,
Like a flower pressed between the pages
Of a book put aside long ago, and reopened
At the beginning of the unread final chapter.

Phil

The plum-lacquered woven Japanese basket Phil
    lately back from Kyoto gave us,
        Juliet's baby bed on Nymph & Cherry
The year Phil dwelt over on Larch with Don
Beyond the shimmering silver dollar eucalypti,
Sometimes strolled two dirt road blocks to visit,
People mad at him if he came over, if he didn't
    he later recollected.
Toting his laundry downtown, two sad sacks.
Later on camped down on Terrace tender
    dear heart crotchety and alone
In the same town with the vivacious Muse
Not quite on the outs & not quite on the ins with her,
    impatient
    amid nasturtiums
One day on acid sternly informed me, Thomas Clark,
Poetry will never get written this way.

All

for Robert Creeley (1926–2005)

With Bob and Joanne then, rounding
the cliffs from Wharf Road
to the beach one idle late summer
afternoon, as if time were endless,
sitting down then to rest
as if at home, at water's

edge, the seabirds swooping,
the beach empty, the talk lapping,
inconsequential, nothing brings
consequence, all happens, all this
sweet nothing. The moments flood back,
a blurring tide, and then withdraw

again into the ever
accumulating pool of ebbing
attentions, lost hopes, forgotten so
called dreams. No longer here to live,
simply to snatch another breath.
Three sat talking on the beach, one

doesn't know what was meant,
one doesn't know what was
said. But the faces, the voices
come for a moment clear. There, in
that light. Here. The tide incoming.
So it was then as the sun went down.

Memories at Dawn

to Ryan Newton

another sleepless night
castaway tears
lost own worlds
never stop
remembered moments
wasted years—winter morning
in the dark
cat snoring
before dawn
memories
at random—stupid
clean white
cold kitchen
outside Paw Paw
Michigan
Saturday (barren)
late autumn
1940s
(barren days)
boy with radio
alone
Everett Sonny Grandelius
running wild
for Spartans

against green
giant Irish
Ryan
the personal means
nothing
without pause
no intervals
all flows
rushing toward the end
orphaned history
down by the barn
mother cat gone hunting
her squealing kittens
drowned
in a milk can
under the closed lid
of a metal urn
filled with water
without pause
"Uncle Jack
  & Aunt Sadie's"
  though not related
  no blood in those veins
  1940s
  city boy with radio
  alone
  down on the farm
  ah the lonely
  vacant

trustlessness
of the child
—the resignation
of an abandoned town
in a dead
quiet nation
as yet unborn

Ann Arbor 1960

These then were the green years. Braving the sharp
Bite of the January gale
To eight o'clock Greek class,
From East Ann Street, chap-cheeked
With frozen nostrils and ears.
And then in May the sudden spring
A bath of lilacs and the singing
Of the blood again on dark
Rich nights, alone along the Huron,
A train whistle and strangers involved
In violent argument in a car,
Mysterious, unintelligible
Augury of what would in grey years follow.

At Life

I am no good, nor, I have to allow,
Are many others so much better at it
That I might learn to be good from them.
And besides it's too late now for the blind
Clown to take up the scholar's hornbook
As he pedals off the unobserved cliff.
"I've worn the dress in this role long enough,"
  Says the speech balloon that suspends him,
"To know how to catch the wind in it
  And on this billowing chute to float me down
Gently to touch the fathomless drink
  Upon which the dying sun breathes its meanings,
Shadows born yesterday to die tomorrow—"
The ice shelf collapsed, the dust cloud swiftly coming.

The Key

Does any of the meaning you think at times you see
disappearing ahead of you just out of your reach
actually materialize once you're gone (no longer looking)
Long white nights insomniac alone save
for your stupid fears dull recursive woes inventories
of chronic fuckups defects in the code the world
cup flickering mute on nocturnal tube midnight
to zombie dawn (get a life) later back to books
Henry IV Part One Falstaff a recognizable
human like you takes bribes carries bottle
into battle not gun dismisses honor as a mere
word empty and then Tacitus on globalization
in Britain 2000 years ago the legions of Rome
raptores orbis plunderers of earth prophetic world
dot com fable of profit motive (what else is new)
Then as sun comes up Sunday paper for the obits
wherein growing older you discover your familiars
today Jean du Lac master of the orotone (photo repro
on glass) born in France died in San Francisco ashes
scattered off Marin coast "The majority of his life
a mystery" he "left behind a single key
to a solitary padlock The location of the padlock
is unknown"

Lullaby for Cuckoo

Did you suffer, or was it just the one who made you?
Little bird, deluded or self-deluded,
close your eyes, and let these chirps resound
mechanically. Was vision the clue you lacked,
when emerging from the works you sang sweetly
of midnight, though it was purple noon
and purple riot ran through you, while
the big hand batted and rocked around
the clock, and you alone had time for me?
Or was homo faber the missing link
who forged you in his workshop of stupid toys?
Either way, the little hand is catching up,
the door is opening; you aren't coming out.

A Fairy Tale

The ambassador to the hall of mirrors
Losing himself in troubled reflections shows
His cards against a green felt field of chance:
One turns the page over—how will it come out?—
This formal dance of a tale in need of
A fairy tale ending, starting with a dream,
The storied ball in which the princess
Prepares to die of heartbreak when the music
That rings against the painted sky and tree
Has ceased and the ball is over, finishes
Instead in accident not tragedy,
The bright life in the dark half-life memorized,
The sole remaining sound quiet tires leaving,
The guests' faces pressed to the iced windows,
The long black sigh of the departing diplomat—
Deep in a time that's independent of us
Where that music long ago stopped echoing—
Spiraling like a stopped scream through the blind elms.

Les Etoiles

These globes of gold, islands of light,
sought by the eye in dreams,
flash up from fugitive shadow
glittering dust on the roads of night,

and the breath of evening dying
blows them away

Night Sky

for Blanqui

The universe as the site of lingering cosmic
catastrophes—points of conflict in the text,
                            Nablus, Jenin,
through which it's impossible to see the stars.
Dark spots that shade the eyes. "This eternity
of the human being among the stars is a melancholy
thing . . . There exists a world where a man follows a
road that, in the other world, his double did not take."

The routinization of the suffering that comes with
having a soul. The martyr's pain is repeated in
the same moment over and over again at infinite sites
scattered through the universe, pockets of darkness between stars.

Life as the monotonous flow of an hourglass
that eternally empties and turns itself over, teaching
yes, but always the same lesson, the new sand is
always old the old sand always new.

Hazard Response

As in that grey exurban wasteland in *Gatsby*
When the white sky darkens over the city
Of ashes, far from the once happy valley,
This daze spreads across the blank faces
Of the inhabitants, suddenly deprived
Of the kingdom's original promised gift.
Did I say kingdom when I meant place
Of worship? Original when I meant
Damaged in handling? Promised when
I meant stolen? Gift when I meant
Trick? Inhabitants when I meant slaves?
Slaves when I meant clowns
Who have wandered into test sites? Test
Sites when I meant contagious hospitals?
Contagious hospitals when I meant clouds
Of laughing gas? Laughing gas
When I meant tears? No, it's true,
No one should be writing poetry
In times like these, Dear Reader,
I don't have to tell you of all people why.
It's as apparent as an attempted
Punch in the eye that actually
Catches only empty air—which is
The inside of your head, where
The green ritual sanction
Of the poem has been cancelled.

The Pilots

Ziad Jarrah danced at his female cousin's
Wedding. Slender with glasses, intelligent
Looking, a seemingly happy young man,
Smiling pleasantly, his arms waving in the festive air.

Having lost his son, Mohammed Atta's
Father rages against the Americans. Mohammed's
Boyhood friend weeps to recall the "delicate,
Innocent, virgin" youth of their childhood hours.

Marwan Al-Shehhi lived behind that gate
Between the two buildings, see that obscured
Back yard, where the street starts to get real
Ramshackle—dedicated, serious, committed to the cause.

The standing pool of language, thickened then with
The algae and flotsam of guilt and time
And fear, coagulating to clog
The throat; the conscience anyway never clear . . .

How to build sentences of such transparency
The strange accidence of those pictures of the dead
Peels away to reveal a grammar of humanness
Life our school, knowledge of suffering our teacher.

November of the Plague Year

Unwilling to turn and glimpse the blind exorcist's face,
Unconditional suspenders of disbelief,
Back-to-Normals shop to live, drive to shop

So a busy world spins by my window again
Till buying hour stops, and night noise
Falls through the white rain and hangs there.

Sky glows red with last few searching tracer lights,
Infant tenement memories and other spectral
Mystery silhouettes, shifting in the mind

Between the first and last breaths, a blank disassembling.
Between the first flashback—a brick airshaft,
Carlight Zero diving, wartime voices distant—

And the evaporation of the tribe, replaying
The great mobilization of ghosts
In the grey area, somewhere before dawn.

How long? The shadow of a doubt moves
Across a door in the imagined dark
Of the ancient cranium, under a patriot sky.

Everything Makes Sense If You
Close Your Eyes and Let It

No one upholds a vague ideal better than its victim

The girl volunteer at ground zero who found Osama sexy

And wanted to insinuate herself within those mysterious robes

Pointed up the contradictions of the ethos,

The way isolated individuals within a system

Behave constitutes the rules of the game,

The ritual sanction of the poem demands a forgetting

Of everything the previous lines have implied,

There's nothing so strange about a building flying into a plane.

Halloween of Double Happiness

Mall hunting time spook hovering above
This fete of ghosts, sleuth, sad witness, calm spy,
O moon who's never the same spectator twice
On this Halloween of Double Happiness
Look down on these Scream clones, Uncle Sams, Osamas,
Trawl milky mousefur October for clues,
Peer through a suspicious terra lattice
Upon ritual maskings of grim auspice
And tell us, is this stuff really fun any more?

Lustration Rite

Saturday night kitties loll about bathing
in milky blue flickering TV light and shade
as if it were not the end of the world after all
chimneysweep girl Dark Sister furiously
pecking at herself then abruptly pausing
to stare off into deep space quizzical while
Princey the great sleek black head potentate
laps daintily at his own snowy breastfur
and glances up through slit eyes sphinxlike
across the temple of the disinterested moment
at the advertised world apocalypse

9/29/01

Nux

Little Prince basks serene
As an Egyptian god on his barge
On the green cushion, gently breathing

While in his sleep mouselike plays the mind
With its empty toys less real
Than the large drops of rain the nightwind tosses

The night, dark as the flooding of the Nile
The brain, that clouded crystal ball
Blurry with drowned thoughts—

A waterlogged squirrel that gathers
Its nuts to float this dream of words sub noctis
From *magic* to *error,* from *aether* to *terra*

On the upriver stream toward morning

The Great Sphinx Who Rests With Paws

"Cats allow us to share our lives with them, and in return, share their lives with us. The burden is ours for the joy and privilege."
—FRED SMITH

The great Sphinx who rests solemn and enigmatic with paws folded
    across his beauteous white breast
Mister Twister who astonishingly back-flexes his neck as if upon a
    swivel so as the better to rearward gaze with benign wondering eyes
Moonface Boy whose large round head contains sublunar thoughts
    sly and ever fleeting
Big Penguin whose excellent black and white coat is made more
    splendid by careful grooming and whose intricate and industrious
    pedicures are a thing of joy
Big Panda nuzzling shyly with snout and head butts and bumps and
    cuddles for those he loves
Big Bounder who comes running and leaps headlong upon tables and
    through doorways
Old Cow able to jump over the moony night at will
Society Boy who always wants to keep his friends company and whose
    friends never want to say goodbye
Big Giant whose noble girth daily inspires big hugs and soft words of
    admiration and endearment
Snowy Belly Boy who gazes at you slowly blinking as if from another
    world
Little Prince whose body lies wrapped in roses under cold moonlight
    beneath the dying plum tree beside the bones of Prince Marcel

Empty Message File

those great imploring soulful eyes
your windows on this world

your gaze once serene and benign
now wary and unknowing

whether or not I want to let you go
you are going

     *

farewell sweet prince
beauty sweetness life

it's harvest time
forgive me for having held you so long
(in my fallow field)

Species

Self reborn as lotus in head

better late than never low in the southwest

the full moon a half degree wide
                   just after sunset peeping

        later still, indigo cheesecloth night

Redwood cloaked in fog
raccoons moving from floor to floor,
        from room to room
in the fog,

with a sound like thin paper tearing.

All Souls Night

Tears in the rain
for the sickly lioness with AIDS
and her scrawny, starving cubs
the final understanding too late
       biophilia
emotional need to affiliate
with the rest of the living world
          as it disappears
vs. shrinkage of nature everyday abetted
by cognitive disconnection
            Princey
sprawled asleep sleek
      silky & fat as the night jungle
maybe the last
big cats would make better gods
& goddesses
        than men & women

by the shores of the lakes
       of Africa
emaciated and covered with living sores

The Vacant Estate

The estate stands vacant: the silent stone dogs,
The lawns well grassed, the checkered polyanthus,
The polished porphyry, and—thus
The fool's delusion of an opening—
All the machines are running. It appears
They have simply turned them on and gone.
The coral root oozes syrup sharp as quince,
Jasmine clings to the perspiring palms,
By the rock silverlings glide belly up.
In your dream all the machines are running
(Can they be turned off?) out of the empty house
Across the emerald turf toward you,
Tridents waving like wild stalks of corn,
Antennae scraping the clouds . . . and then they're gone.
You turn around and it's tomorrow,
Nature has shut her doors.

Chiasmus

Black doldrums, then a stir, then tackle snapping—
Which would you prefer, the calm after, during
Or before the storm? Anxious news flutters
Its broadsides across our ragged, tattered
Sails; lightning darkens, and it rains more
Than if the sun, drunk the night before,
Staggered by a wave, fell below the hatches;
While the moon, tossed overboard, washed ashore
On that island which no sailor reaches,
Returns to haunt our sea-locked ship, and night
Comes back to unsettle restive stagnant day.
A rotten state, finally, bearded by flies,
Dogged by the death of the wind at noon
And the breathless simoon at evening;
Black doldrums, then a stir, then tackle snapping.

White Dove

My white dove lies broken
They've taken her into the cave of cold machines
And crushed her wing
Beneath black metal she lies immobilized
Tomorrow the sky will open again
To receive her
There is an awakening a keen
And fresh sense of things
But no one's here to feel it
I've gone up on the roof to look up and wait
For the rain to begin
With these sounds
The black gnashing of a cloud against
The cloud ceiling
The blind flapping of a wing
Against the netting of the cage

The Maid

Your body was my church
and when I made love to you
it was my prayer
sang the deranged monk

I was silent but not alone
in the depths of silence
there is always oneself

The court sat
and when the books were opened
out leapt the flames

A flock of red and yellow birds
thrown
against the grieving clouds
lit up the dying afternoon
like a tear from her eye

Beauty

The fading strains of the dying refrain
warbled by the teakettle to the timeless beauty
who spends her time in the mind that ocean
closed off from us
brought back to her through the shadows of the afternoon
a thought that might have interested us
had we but known it

Prophet

So then he wandered out into the street and began to testify
Something about life being a long journey of the soul
An endless voyaging turning into a voyaging with an end
One knows how but one does not know when
No one yet knows when as the traffic bore down on him

As the traffic bore down on him my mind drifted in the wilderness
Or was it that my mind having been adrift all along
I've just grown to regard the wilderness as my resting or laughing place
He cried but those were not yet his last words
As the traffic parted around him as around one charmed

Adversary

Echoes rebound in the ancient ball court
Against the wind singing in the trees
There is a silent helmetted adversary
Flames glimmer from his deep eye slots

Moths swirl upon glass as if to speak
One sits solitary by the lamp hour by hour
The gleam that keeps the night awake falters
Time as it passes fills up with something else

Invisible gaps open to the past
The clock does not strike as expected
The cavalcade has dispersed without lament
Words have been forsaken by their letters

But day and night still struggle on
And though day noisily contend
At the end shadow stands alone
Masked in the dark clearing waiting

The Two Lords

On a golden dais laid over broken stones in the declining shadow
Between the rising of the Evening Star and the setting of the Morning
    Star
In the time of the invader the time of the Smoking Mirror the time of
    Burning Water
When each must embrace the fate that has been coded
Two battle-clad chiefs meet to wrangle over cosmic strategy
Lord One offers the hand of war a lifted fist with index finger upraised
Lord Two offers the hand of submission an open palm extended
The two lords their attitudes fixed unchanging in the foretime
Unchanging in the afterlife as in this life through which we
    must yet live

As If Anything Could Happen

At a dark portal between cosmic realms
A wizard found himself stood up by the Morning Star—
Evening his element as the Rain God's is water.

She who has the power of giving flowers
Promises everything is alive to the world
As long as the night sky stays fresh and new.

But if the Moon Goddess drown in a waterlily
And burning clouds fall in a heavy curtain
On dry leaves drifting and blowing over blue sands

Her low pressing voice will disturb the wind
With troubled words to which the Morning Star
Must attend—leaving that patient wizard

In the dark, his element as the Death God's
Is earth—he who has awaited her
Since the Time God first bent under

His long miscalculation of numbers and years
Now arrayed again in night tracer fire over Fallujah
Like a cold conflagration of Northern Lights.

In the Time of the Smoking Mirror

A heaven invented as supposed
for the benefit and solace
of the dispossessed, but

always occupied in fact
by the rich—the chiefs, and those
with the best tricks—

"Only a moment here on earth.
It is untrue that we have come
to live here on earth."

The hand and foot prints on the rock suggest
the presence of unseen
beings who have been here

before us. The air, god-charged.
The words, cut from the same stone
that will lie over us,

have been given only a moment
to prepare that place to
which we have been sent.

Post-Election

after Baudelaire's Fusées

The world's just about done. The only reason for it to keep on going is the fact that it exists. What a lame reason, given the far better reasons to the contrary. What's there left for it to do? Even if it managed to go on materially existing, would this existence be worth a shit? Who'd be interested in its history? I'm not saying everything will collapse and we'll wander the ruins, hunting down our next meals: No way, we're too feeble, we've lost whatever energies once may have enabled a hand-to-mouth life. The world has become too Americanized for that. The American idea of progress has atrophied the spirit of the world. We dream our brilliant utopias, our conquests of nature, our marvelous religious wars. The outcome will betray the dream. You who consider yourself intelligent, tell me what's really left of life. Spare me the display of your devotions to the relics of your beliefs—to perform them is to renounce their intended objects. Our claim to earth ended with the decline of primogeniture. What will be left for the eldest son, no longer the elected one, to do, save to exact revenge by stealing the sustenance of hungry young animals? But even that won't be the worst thing that happens.

The Course of Empire Unwinds

Two hundred millennia and to set foot out of Africa the first mistake
Since then night border patrolling and the whacking of unfamiliars

The work of all those years spent attaching oneself to a tree
The effacing of the white sails that crossed the first prairie

A thousand days glittering with blood in the glass cities
Gem engorged carved amber arcades

Ignored by wave after wave of blind invaders
Evening prepares their ceremonial tombs in sacred waters

Decanted from the lake of black stars and sunken plunder
Its messages rising before them in the false atoms of dreams

Sunflowers

A clear night sky steeped in blue and green starlight
Hollow and deep as a huge sea shell flushed from within
And reddening as the rising god once again commands
The drowsy sunflowers to lift their heads and open their black eyes

Teaches us how the world begins all over the earth
How to greet one another in language beyond words
To depart unconcerned with any idea of return and perhaps
To at last begin to speak without not thinking

Selected Bibliography

POETRY

Airplanes (Once, 1966)

The Sand Burg (Ferry, 1966)

Bun (with Ron Padgett) (Angel Hair, 1968)

Stones (Harper & Row, 1969)

Chicago (with Lewis Warsh) (Angel Hair, 1969)

Air (Harper & Row, 1970)

Green (Black Sparrow, 1971)

Neil Young (Coach House, 1971)

John's Heart (Goliard/Grossman, 1972)

Smack (Black Sparrow, 1972)

Blue (Black Sparrow, 1974)

At Malibu (Kulchur, 1975)

35 (Poltroon, 1976)

Fan Poems (North Atlantic, 1976)

How I Broke In (Tombouctou, 1977)

The Mutabilitie of the English Lyrick (Poltroon, 1978)

When Things Get Tough on Easy Street: Selected Poems 1963–1978
    (Black Sparrow, 1978)

The End of the Line (Little Caesar, 1980)

A Short Guide to the High Plains (Cadmus, 1981)

Nine Songs (Turkey, 1981)

Under the Fortune Palms (Turkey, 1982)

Paradise Resisted: Selected Poems 1978–1984 (Black Sparrow, 1984)

The Border (Coffee House, 1985)

Disordered Ideas (Black Sparrow, 1987)

Apocalyptic Talkshow (Bloody Twin, 1987)

His Supposition (Werkman, 1987)

Easter Sunday (Coffee House, 1988)

Fractured Karma (Black Sparrow, 1990)

Sleepwalker's Fate: New and Selected Poems 1965–1991 (Black
    Sparrow, 1992)

Junkets on a Sad Planet: Scenes from the Life of John Keats (Black
    Sparrow, 1994)

Like Real People (Black Sparrow, 1995)

Empire of Skin (Black Sparrow, 1997)

White Thought (Hard Press/The Figures, 1997)

Cold Spring: A Diary (Skanky Possum, 2000)

Zombie Dawn (with Anne Waldman) (Skanky Possum, 2003)

Night Sky (Deep Forest, 2004)

Threnody (effing, 2006)

FICTION

Who Is Sylvia? (Blue Wind, 1979)

The Last Gas Station and Other Stories (Black Sparrow, 1980)

Heartbreak Hotel (Coffee House, 1981)

The Exile of Céline (Random House, 1987)

The Spell: A Romance (Black Sparrow, 2000)

BIOGRAPHY

Champagne and Baloney: The Rise and Fall of Finley's A's (Harper
    & Row, 1976)

No Big Deal (with Mark Fidrych) (Lippincott, 1977)

The World of Damon Runyon (Harper & Row, 1978)

One Last Round for The Shuffler (Truck/Pomerica, 1979)

Jack Kerouac (Harcourt Brace Jovanovich, 1984)

Late Returns: A Memoir of Ted Berrigan (Tombouctou, 1985)

Kerouac's Last Word: Jack Kerouac in Escapade (Water Row, 1986)

Charles Olson: The Allegory of a Poet's Life (Norton, 1991)

Robert Creeley and the Genius of the American Common Place (New Directions, 1993)

Things Happen for a Reason: The True Story of an Itinerant Life in Baseball (with Terry Leach) (Frog, 2000)

Edward Dorn: A World of Difference (North Atlantic, 2002)

POLEMIC

The Great Naropa Poetry Wars (Cadmus, 1980)

ART

Baseball (The Figures, 1976)

DRAMA

The Emperor of the Animals (Goliard, 1967)

LITERARY ESSAYS

The Poetry Beat: Reviewing the Eighties (University of Michigan, 1990)

Acknowledgments

Many of the poems in this book appeared previously in volumes listed in the Selected Bibliography.

Some of the recent poems first appeared in *The American Poetry Review, Beatitude, Bombay Gin, Columbia Poetry Review, Crab Orchard Review, Divide, 88, House Organ, Indiana Review, Jacket, March Magazine, Milk, Mississippi Review, Night Palace, Noi, Noigandres/Deep Forest Review, Ploughshares, Skanky Possum, Square One, Tight, Transit, Van Gogh's Ear, Woodstock Journal, Weigh Station*, and *ZYZZYVA*.

"All Thought" appeared as an Auguste Press broadside.

"Hazard Response" appeared as a 911 Camelia St. broadside.

"All Souls Night" appeared as a Noigandres Press broadside.

"The Pilots" appeared in *September 11: West Coast Writers Approach Ground Zero* (Hawthorne Books).

"Lullaby for Cuckoo" appeared in *The Best American Poetry 2002*, ed. Robert Creeley (Scribner's).

"Phil" appeared in *Continuous Flame: A Tribute to Philip Whalen*, ed. Michael Rothenberg and Suzi Winson (Fish Drum).

"Nux" appeared in *180 More Extraordinary Poems for Every Day*, ed. Billy Collins (Random House).

"Prophet" and "Elegy" appeared in *The Oxford Book of American Poetry*, ed. David Lehman (Oxford University Press).

Biographical and bibliographical information about Tom Clark, including an interview concerning this book, can be found at:
http://jacketmagazine.com/bio/clark-t.html

COLOPHON

Light & Shade was designed at Coffee House Press in the historic warehouse district of downtown Minneapolis. The text is set in Minion.

FUNDER ACKNOWLEDGMENTS

Coffee House Press is an independent nonprofit literary publisher. Our books are made possible through the generous support of grants and gifts from many foundations, corporate giving programs, individuals, and through state and federal support. This book received special project support from an anonymous donor. Coffee House Press receives general operating support from the Minnesota State Arts Board, through an appropriation by the Minnesota State Legislature and from the National Endowment for the Arts, a federal agency. Coffee House receives major funding from the McKnight Foundation, and from Target. Coffee House also receives significant support from: the Buuck Family Foundation; the Bush Foundation; the Patrick and Aimee Butler Family Foundation; Consortium Book Sales and Distribution; the Foundation for Contemporary Arts; Stephen and Isabel Keating; the Outagamie Foundation; the Pacific Foundation, the law firm of Schwegman, Lundberg, Woessner & Kluth, P.A.; the James R. Thorpe Foundation; the Archie D. and Bertha H. Walker Foundation; TLR/West; the Woessner Freeman Family Foundation; and many other generous individual donors.

This activity is made possible in part by a grant from the Minnesota State Arts Board, through an appropriation by the Minnesota State Legislature and a grant from the National Endowment for the Arts.

MINNESOTA STATE ARTS BOARD

TARGET.

To you and our many readers across the country,
we send our thanks for your continuing support.

Good books are brewing at coffeehousepress.org

TOM CLARK has worked as a writer, editor, and critic of poetry for over forty years. He has published many collections of poems and received awards for his poetry from the Rockefeller and Guggenheim Foundations as well as the National Endowment for the Arts. He served as poetry editor of *The Paris Review* (1963–1973) and, in the 1980s and 1990s, as a poetry critic for *The Los Angeles Herald Examiner, Los Angeles Times,* and *San Francisco Chronicle.* He has also written a number of critical biographies, including lives of Jack Kerouac, Charles Olson, Ted Berrigan, Robert Creeley, and Edward Dorn. For the past twenty years he has been a core faculty member and lecturer in Poetics for New College of California.